D0283772

living with less

Date: 3/5/12

241.4 TAB
Tabb, Mark A.
Living with less: the upside of
downsizing your life /

PALM BEACH COUNTY
LIBRARY SYSTEM
3650 SUMMIT BLVD.
WEST PALM BEACH, FL 33406

mark tabb

living with less

the upside of
downsizing your life

B&H
PUBLISHING GROUP
NASHVILLE, TENNESSEE

© 2006 by Mark Tabb
All rights reserved
Printed in the United States of America

ISBN: 978-0-8054-3296-1

Published by B & H Publishing Group,
Nashville, Tennessee

Dewey Decimal Classification: 248.84
Subject Heading: CHRISTIAN LIFE \ BIBLE. N.T. MARK
                  MATERIALISM

Unless noted otherwise, scriptural passages are from the Holman Christian Standard Bible, © 1999, 2000, 2002, 2003 by Holman Bible Publishers, Nashville Tennessee; all rights reserved. Other translations quoted are NCV, the Holy Bible, New Century Version, © 1987, 1988, 1991 by Word Publishing, Dallas, Texas 75039, all rights reserved; NIV, the Holy Bible, New International Version, © 1973, 1978, 1984 by International Bible Society; NLT, the Holy Bible, New Living Translation, ©1996, used by permission of Tyndale House Publishers Inc., Wheaton, Illinois 60189, all rights reserved; MSG, The Message: The Bible in Contemporary Language, copyright 2002 by Eugene Peterson, Navpress, all rights reserved; TLB, The Living Bible, copyright 1971, used by permission of Tyndale House Publishers Inc., Wheaton, Illinois 60189, all rights reserved.

6 7 8 9 10 11 12 13 14 15 16   14 13 12 11 10

For Valerie

Contents

More from Less

*L*et me get right to the point: The only way to get more out of life is to choose less.

Less stuff.

Less activity.

Less wanting more.

Less of you.

I apologize if this seems a little abrupt. Believe me, I searched for a different way to kick this off. I wanted to ease into the heavy stuff to make it more palatable and less offensive. Still, more than once, I found myself hitting the Delete button on a touching story because "touching" and "heartwarming" didn't quite fit.

I also thought it might be easier if some famed contemplative hit you with the bad news. Maybe Saint Augustine wouldn't insult you while telling you all your priorities are wrong, that you've wasted your life in your pursuit of comfort and material goods. Perhaps you wouldn't be angry if C. S. Lewis told you the frustration that fills your life will never go away until you slow down and begin saying no to yourself and your children. And if Mr. Rogers confronted you with your need to crawl out of the center of your universe and assume a lifestyle of humility, who could argue?

So I searched my library for just the right quote from my favorite authors. One or two came close, but I thought it better just to come right out and say what you and I need to hear: The key to making life matter is to choose to live with less.

Give stuff away.

Simplify your lifestyle.

Deflate your opinion of yourself.

Choose less because less is more.

There I go again, writing with a two-by-four. I keep trying to stop. A wise man once said the bruises of a friend are better than the kisses of an enemy, and that's what I'm trying to do: bruise my friends, beginning with myself. I don't enjoy the process, but there is no other way. The bruises on my forehead are starting to add up, but I can't help myself. I've reached a point where the pain is better than the delusion that I can have it all and still have my life count for something. For too long I've spiritualized the hard sayings of Jesus and Moses and Solomon. I know real life is not measured by how much I own, but I assumed I could own as much as I wanted as long as I kept everything in its proper perspective.

I can't. None of us can.

We can't because the world of work and school and mortgages and loading kids in the minivan for ball practice and band recitals and school open houses leaves little time for anything else. The psalmist said to be still and know that the Lord is God, but stillness is hard to find in the perpetual-motion machine in which most of us live. Jesus said He came that you and I might have life and have it to the full. My life is full. Yours probably is as well. Too full. Full of stuff. Full of activities. Full of ever-expanding schedules and shrinking days. Full of the desire for more. Somehow, I don't believe this is what Jesus had in mind. Through it all, something is missing. And that something is the very thing I really want out of life.

I want joy. Not happiness, but real abiding joy—a joy that outlasts hard times and refuses to be chained to good times.

I want real relationships. I know a lot of people. I want to really know some of them, beginning with my family.

I want freedom. Not the freedom to do what I want, but the freedom to go to sleep at night without the weight of worry raising my blood pressure.

But more than anything, I want what I devote my life to, to last longer than I do.

Unfortunately, all I really want out of life is constantly squeezed out by noises that refuse to take no for an answer. The bills, they demand to be paid. They get really angry when they're ignored. And food, everyone in my household has this strange addiction to food. Someone has to go buy it. Someone has to prepare it. Someone has to clean up afterward. If only the Little Red Hen were available. And the house, it always wants something. "Mow my yard," it says. "And clean my gutters and fix my roof and unclog my sink." The house never shuts up (although I learned a long time ago to tune out its demand to be cleaned). And I'm just getting started.

Then there's the rush. It never seems to end. Between the job and the kids and church, there's never a moment to call our own. Even if we did, it isn't as though our minds would be free to focus on what we really want out of life.

The only thing better than the rush is stress-filled rush. And stress is everywhere. Especially at work. If by some strange coincidence we managed to have a stress-free day on the job, the world might come to an end. Someone always has a complaint or the boss wants to downsize manpower while increasing production or rumors of a merger and subsequent job cuts float around. If everybody I worked with weren't so—how can I put this mildly?—common sense-challenged and if they would just stop griping for even a day, maybe then I could make a serious run at joy or real relationships or doing something that will outlast me. But they don't and I can't and I wonder if I ever will.

And home isn't much better. The average family is always on the run. This conglomeration of people who love one another rarely finds time to eat a meal together. And with each passing year, it seems to get worse. Too much to do, too little time—"intimate strangers" may be a better label than "family."

I look for a little solace at church, but between committee meetings and Bible study groups and taking the youth bowling and working on the building (which wasn't built right to begin with, so much for quality work from volunteers), the place sometimes gives me more headaches than peace and joy and love. Then the pastor asks for volunteers for a new program he wants to start. I know I should sign up, but I don't want to give up another Saturday. Instead of feeling better about my life, I walk away feeling guilty.

Now that my whine fest is over, can I be completely honest? The demands and stress of the day rarely keep me from pursuing deeper relationships with my wife and daughters. My job doesn't rob me of time I might spend on the things that are most important to me. Mowing the lawn and painting doors and all the constant maintenance my one-hundred-year-old house demands never stop me from doing what I want to do. No, the greatest barrier I must overcome in my struggle to find the life I really want is me. And your greatest barrier is you.

I know what I say I want out of life. With my lips I confess that joy is found in growing closer to people I love and becoming more like the God I say I follow. But when push comes to shove, I shove myself onto the couch, remote in hand, and waste hours at a time, ignoring both my God and my family. I know with my head that money can't buy happiness, but that doesn't stop me from drooling over the Best Buy ads. And then there's the schedule. No one makes us try to do it all. Running children from one event or practice to another until we identify the days of the week by the coach we see is not forced upon us. The pressure comes from within. From inside of me. I could say no. And so could you. But we don't. We can't. Somehow the incredible pace of our schedule meets a need. It makes us feel important, useful. Again, the problem isn't the coach who calls and asks if I can make twenty-five sandwiches for the track team. The real problem is me.

My life and my schedule and my stress didn't choose me. I chose them. Before I can even think of trying to squeeze more joy out of life, I must first realize that something has to change. Only when I reach the point of frustration meltdown—when I go to bed and wonder where the day went and dread dragging myself out from under the covers in six hours—only then will I be willing to make some needed changes.

And that's what this book is all about. This isn't a book that will tell you how to squeeze more out of an already-packed schedule. Nor will it tell you how to find both material comfort and spiritual bliss. You will not find the path to the simple life in which you and your family will live in perfect peace and harmony. I wish you could, but perfect peace and harmony cannot be found this side of heaven. Instead, this is a book about making one of the most difficult decisions any of us will ever make—the decision to choose less out of life so that you might find what you really want. The only way to enjoy life is to choose to live with less, for less is more.

What follows are not some pie-in-the-sky platitudes discovered while spending a couple of years holed up in some desert monastery. Nor are the following sixteen chapters full of perfected advice. More than anything I've ever written, this book has been a journey. I started working on the idea more than five years ago. As time passed, I assumed that moving from a concept to words on a page would be easy. After all, I felt like I'd lived the tough choices this book challenges you to make. And then I started writing. I discovered I had so much more to learn.

What follows is the most difficult book I've ever attempted—a fact I find more than a little ironic. A book on simplifying life complicated my own life as I tried to write it. Now, looking back over the process of the past few months, I realize it had to be this way. Choosing less in a world that refuses to deny itself anything will never be easy. Ever. Nor did I want to paint the picture of some ideal life with clichéd solutions that would only leave you frustrated and burdened with guilt. This world is a complicated place and has been since the day Adam and Eve disobeyed God and plunged the world into sin. Finding our way through this mess will not be easy.

Finally, I wanted this book to accurately reflect the message of the Bible. Real life can only be found in a right relationship with the God who created you. I pray that message flows through every page.

The only way to get more out of life is to choose less. Less stuff. Less activity. Less wanting more. Less of you. And less of me too. May God give us the courage to choose less so that we might experience more of the life He has planned for us.

Smaller

Chapter 1

So What Do You Want out of Life?

*It is vanity to wish for long life
and to care little about a well-spent life.*
THOMAS À KEMPIS, *THE IMITATION OF CHRIST*

||||||||||||||||||||||||||||||||||||||||||||||||||||

*He has planted eternity in the human heart,
but even so, people cannot see the whole scope
of God's work from beginning to end.*
ECCLESIASTES 3:11 (NLT)

*N*obody ever says, "I want to throw my life away." At least not in words. You never hear a commencement speaker challenge graduates to go out into the world and fritter away their lives on trivialities that evaporate from memory five seconds after they're done. Some speakers may want to, but no one ever does. Nor does anyone ever plan to have the words "Who cares who lies here? He didn't do much anyway" etched on their tombstone. We'd rather donate our bodies to science than leave behind a legacy of absolute uselessness. At least then our corpse might serve some greater purpose. No one wants to live a life that is pointless. Our

3

souls are hardwired for something more. We want to find some reason for our existence. We need our lives to matter.

We also feel compelled to find happiness. We want to smile. We want to laugh. We want to enjoy the time we have on planet Earth. Every fairy tale ends with the words, "And they lived happily ever after," and that's what we hope to find as well—the happy ending, along with the happy beginning and happy middle. Happiness is more than a goal. We regard it as a God-given right. The Declaration of Independence itself calls the pursuit of happiness one of the inalienable rights endowed by our Creator, along with life and liberty. And pursue it we do. We choose everything from careers to mates to fabric softeners based on what will make us happy. Although we soon learn that we can't be happy every minute of every day, we hope the good times will outnumber the bad. We want the same for our children and grandchildren. Just let them be happy and healthy, and we will be satisfied.

That's all we really want out of life: a reason for living and a way to enjoy the journey. Is that too much to ask?

Standing in Our Way

Perhaps it is too much to ask. The world in which we live is not designed to foster happiness. Danger lurks around every corner, while pain and suffering hunt us down like hungry lions. No one is exempt. There is no safe place to hide, no little patch of unspoiled paradise that will etch permanent smiles on our faces.

My wife and I thought we found a perfect spot early one afternoon while driving along the California coast. We stopped just north of San Francisco at a place called Stinson Beach. To me, the combination of peaks and pines of the mountains with the soft sand, rolling surf, and sea lions of the beach made this place heaven on earth. After buying supplies from a sandwich shop for a romantic picnic, the two of us walked out across the sand to a deserted spot. No one and nothing could spoil this perfect getaway. Nothing, that is, except every seagull from the Gulf of Alaska to Baja, California.

Apparently, seagulls have a taste for roast beef sandwiches with a light vinaigrette dressing, because approximately half a million of them surrounded us, waiting for us to put the sandwiches on the sand and run for our lives. They kept creeping closer and closer, while letting out little chirps that seemed to say, "Drop the sandwiches and we'll let you out alive." I've seen Hitchcock's *The Birds*. So has my wife. We thought we were about to star in the live version. Needless to say, our picnic didn't go off as planned.

The problem wasn't just the 87 million seagulls visiting Stinson Beach on the same late September afternoon as my wife and I. The problem was and is life. It is not designed to automatically dispense happiness. Seagulls spoil picnics, moths eat wool coats, potholes destroy McPherson struts, and these are just the minor annoyances that make happiness a difficult state to maintain. When life really gets going, happiness quickly gives way to sorrow and despair. I'm not a pessimist—far from it. I'm a realist. And the one inescapable reality none of us can ignore is that we live in a world where everyone dies in the end. As long as that statistic remains unchanged, life can never be completely happy and trouble free.

Nor does this world show us how our lives can matter. When we look at all we accomplish while racing on the treadmill of accumulating stuff and paying bills, it all looks

so futile. The wisest man who ever lived, ancient Israel's
King Solomon, put it this way:
"Everything is meaningless," says the Teacher,
"utterly meaningless!"
What do people get for all their hard work?
Generations come and go, but nothing really
changes. The sun rises and sets and hurries around
to rise again. The wind blows south and north,
here and there, twisting back and forth, getting
nowhere. The rivers run into the sea, but the sea
is never full. Then the water returns again to the
rivers and flows again to the sea. Everything is so
weary and tiresome! No matter how much we see,
we are never satisfied. No matter how much we
hear, we are not content.
History merely repeats itself. It has all been
done before. Nothing under the sun is truly
new. What can you point to that is new? How do
you know it didn't already exist long ago? We don't
remember what happened in those former times.
And in future generations, no one will remember
what we are doing now. (Eccles. 1:2–11 NLT)

That was nice and depressing, but it is also true. I think
the last line is the most telling: "We don't remember what
happened in those former times. And in future generations,
no one will remember what we are doing now." All but one
or two of the billions of people now living on the planet will
be completely forgotten shortly after their deaths. The sum
total of our lives' work will either die with us, or if we do
manage to leave something lasting behind, our contribution
to it will soon fade from memory.

I know there are exceptions to this rule, but they are few and far between. For the rest of us, the life cycle of the average human being goes something like this: we're born, we live, we die, and we're eventually forgotten. End of story. Every generation since the beginning of time has been locked into this unrelenting cycle, and every generation will be until the world ceases to be.

So what's the point of working hard and trying to find some reason for living? When we look only at the physical world that surrounds us, we have to reach the same conclusion Agent Smith uttered in the climatic battle of the *Matrix* trilogy: "The purpose of all life is to end." You don't matter. I don't matter. Nothing matters. Life is nothing more than meaningless existence. When the physical universe is our only frame of reference, what other conclusion can we draw?

Time to Move

We crave meaning and purpose while toiling away in a universe that tells us there is no point except to live and die. We long for happiness in a world filled with pain and sickness and death. Am I the only one who sees the irony in this? Call me crazy, but it looks to me like we're living in the wrong place.

You might say I'm overreacting. *We can't expect life to give us everything we want,* you say, and I agree. *Life is what we make it.* Perhaps, but making it into something worthwhile is an uphill climb. *Happiness is a choice and so is living a life that matters. We find meaning when we choose to give our lives meaning.* Yeah, yeah, yeah, whatever. All the pithy little sayings in the world won't change the fact that we live in a place filled with heartache and pain—a place

7

where nothing lasts, not even you and me. We might feel like we're doing something worthwhile in the work that fills our brief existences, but if our lives' work fades away shortly after we do, does it even matter that we lived?

And yes, I know we can find moments of happiness on this earth. I love those times and am thankful for every one I've ever experienced. But if I live for those moments and make them my sole quest in life, I will die disappointed. Moments of happiness do not last, nor do they completely satisfy the ache within our souls. I can pretend they do, but to do so I must close my eyes to the cruelty of the world around me and ignore the cries of the suffering.

I'm not trying to depress us. After all, you bought this book because it promised to help you bring some order to the chaos of daily life. Telling you life is meaningless and devoid of lasting happiness doesn't exactly sound like the path to a simpler and better life. But it is. Simplicity begins with coming to grips with the true nature of the universe. The best way to get your life under control is to understand that your life needs a change of venue. You and I need to move to a place that can give us what we truly want out of life. As long as the physical universe remains our point of reference, we will never find what we are looking for.

A Place to Call Home

The Bible begins with a very simple statement, "In the beginning God created the heavens and the earth." Everything that follows builds on this one statement. If the first verse of the Bible isn't true, the rest of it is irrelevant and so are our lives. The reason is simple: If God did not create the heavens and the earth, if the physical universe is all there is and all there ever will be, then every possible source of meaning and happiness is just as temporary and arbitrary as the universe itself. All are nothing more than futile attempts to make ourselves feel better. If the universe just happened, it doesn't mean anything and neither do we.

However, if God indeed created the heavens and the earth, the physical universe ceases to be our only frame of reference. We already know the world we can see, smell, taste, and touch has a beginning and will eventually come to an end. It is temporary. But the God who made it exists outside of the prison of time. The world may be temporary, but He is permanent. The Bible goes on to say that not only did God create the heavens and the earth, but He also made you and me *in His image* (Gen. 1:26–27). He didn't do this with any other created being. Neither dolphins nor dachshunds are made in God's image, nor anything in between. God reserved this touch for human beings.

The presence of the image of God within us is why we long for something we cannot find in the world in which we live. When God made us like Himself, He placed a longing for the eternal—that which is permanent—deep within our souls. We're like God in that our frame of reference can never be confined to the physical universe. That longing for lasting happiness and a life that matters is, in reality, the siren song of our true home calling out to us. We will never find what we are looking for until we return there. Going home doesn't mean we first have to die. Instead it means moving our focal point off of the temporary and fixing it upon the eternal. Instead of living for this world that will soon pass away, we live for the eternal world, the realm where God dwells.

I know this sounds a little complicated for a book on simplifying life, but this process of changing the venue in which our lives are lived is much simpler than you might imagine. In fact, this is the first and most important step toward getting your life down to a manageable size. More important, this is the only path that leads to a life that matters.

First Steps

I'm writing this chapter during the black hole on the sports fan's calendar—the two weeks before the Super Bowl. Over the next fourteen days the hype over football's ultimate game will build to a fever pitch. On Sunday the network broadcasting the game will devote twelve hours of airtime to a game that lasts just over three hours. Every player, every coach, every single factor that could decide the outcome of the game will be discussed ad nauseam. There will be slow-motion highlights of both teams' seasons, complete with dramatic music pounding in the background. By the time kickoff rolls around, you would think the fate of the free world stands in the balance. Perhaps it does. After all, what could be more important than winning a championship in the (cue the music) National . . . Football . . . League?! Former Dallas Cowboys running back Duane Thomas, who starred in Super Bowl VI, answered that question more eloquently than I could ever hope to: "If it's the ultimate [game]," he said, "how come they're playing it again next year?"

He's right. How can the Super Bowl be the be-all and end-all of the football universe when they will hold another Super Bowl next year and the year after that and the year after that? Duane Thomas looked through the hype and all the talk of history being made on a football field and saw the ultimate gridiron battle for what it really was: a game. Nothing more. Twenty-two guys, eleven on a side, run around on a one-hundred-yard field for sixty minutes. The winners get a trophy, some rings, and a large check. The losers take home a smaller check but no trophy or rings. People talk about what happened for a few days and then forget about football until the next fall. In the end, Roman numerals notwithstanding, the Super Bowl goes down as just another game.

That same perspective is what we must have to change venues with our lives and start down the path toward a life that matters. God made us for eternity, but we live in a world that is temporary. This means all of the stuff that seems so important here on earth, the decisions that keep us up at night—Pepsi or Coke, Honda or Toyota, paper or plastic—aren't that important after all. What really matters is making your life count both now and forever. Fame, fortune, and power—the three quests for which people will sacrifice anything—appear gargantuan in a world of time, but from the perspective of the King of kings, who spoke all of creation into existence, they are just an illusion. That's why the psalmist said the Lord sits on His throne and laughs at the power mongers on earth and all their vain plots (Ps. 2:2–4).

The same goes for the pursuits that fill the lives of ordinary people like you and me. We spend our lives chasing after bigger houses and fancier cars and high-def plasma televisions with a width measured in feet, not inches—a television with a screen so sharp, you feel like you're sitting at the game! Oops, sorry, visions from Best Buy ads started dancing in my head. All of the stuff that pushes our calendars to the edge doesn't really matter when viewed from an eternal perspective.

We must live in the eternal if we want the time we spend here on earth to matter. Our souls crave happiness, but we end up searching for it in all the wrong places. Somewhere along the way, we believed the lie that what will make us happier is more stuff or more authority or more applause at the end of the PTA fund-raiser we spent so much time organizing. When none of those work, we look for happiness in pleasure, but it doesn't take long to figure out the two don't necessarily go together. It's time to change venues and discover the joy that comes from living a life that counts.

And we search for a way to make our lives matter, yet we're confused on how to make that happen. When we use the scale of time, we end up thinking we have to make our mark on this world in some tangible way. But in the end, the process leaves us frustrated, because real meaning cannot be found in anything this world has to offer. We have to shift our perspective and stop looking in time for what can be discovered only in eternity. As the apostle Paul tells us: "Since you have been raised to new life with Christ, set your sights on the realities of heaven, where Christ sits at God's right hand in the place of honor and power. Let heaven fill your thoughts. Do not think only about things down here on earth. For you died when Christ died, and your real life is hidden with Christ in God" (Col. 3:1–3 NLT).

It All Starts with You

The shift from living for time to living for eternity will change our perspective on the stuff that eventually ends up in a yard sale or on eBay and on ourselves. Looking in the mirror of time, we see ourselves in a whole new light. The problem most of us wrestle with (at least, I know I wrestle with it) is not the shiny new toys that fill the Sunday newspaper ads. The real problem is me. Living in the temporary world skews our perspective from the moment we first become self-aware. The problem is pride. Or more to the point, the problem is self-centeredness. All of us have it. We couch the pursuit in more palatable terms, but every human being wrestles with the desire to place themselves at the center of their own personal universe.

When we shift our gaze from the temporary realm to the realm in which the Lord of the universe reigns, we can see ourselves for who we truly are. We are frail creatures of dust, while God is the Almighty, sovereign Creator. What other choice do we then have but to fall on our knees and humble ourselves before Him? Only then will we begin to move from the world of the temporary to the world that holds all we really want in life. The starting point is humility. We must humble ourselves before God—an action that deflates our opinion of ourselves as we live among other creatures made in His image. Then and only then are we ready to start the process of bringing our lives under control.

The only way to make my life matter is to choose less. And the first thing I need less of is me. Once that issue is settled, I am in a position to live a life that lasts longer than I do.

Chapter 2

Worth the Effort

*I came to realize that life lived to help
others is the only one that matters. This is my
highest and best use as a human.*

BEN STEIN

▬▬▬▬▬▬▬▬▬▬▬▬▬▬▬▬▬▬▬▬▬▬

*Don't worry about everyday life—whether you
have enough food to eat or clothes to wear. For
life consists of far more than food and clothing.*

LUKE 12:22–23 (NLT)

*M*y neighbor recently said, "Hey, Mark, did you notice
the paint is coming off your house?" Of course I'd
noticed. Everyone who drives down our street notices. How
can you miss the odd-shaped white patches on the side of a
house or large sheets of sage green paint lying on the ground?
I wanted to reply, "You mean those white spots aren't supposed to be there?" but I didn't.

My house is shedding like a dog in spring, but only on
one side. The rest of the paint looks like it did the day it was
sprayed on four years ago. Unfortunately, whoever painted
my house a few months before I bought it did not properly
prepare the north side of the structure. He probably didn't
let the wall dry long enough after he power-washed away the

sky-blue paint someone else put on the house years earlier. The residual moisture kept the new paint from sticking, and now I have to paint it again.

Life is like a molting house. Nothing lasts. The paint flakes off or fades away or just wears out. There are no exceptions. Paint doesn't last. Clothes don't last. Cars don't last. People don't last. Everything in the universe is temporary, including you and me. This isn't exactly breaking news. I had this epiphany one Christmas morning when my favorite toy broke less than an hour after I'd unwrapped it. I think I was five at the time. All my toys have been breaking ever since. And so have yours. Some toys last longer than others, but eventually they all give in to the forces of time and decay. That is why deep inside of each one of us lurks a hunger for something permanent—something that won't flake off and fall to the ground.

Even though I know nothing lasts, I still struggle to break completely free of the material world. The new paint I spread on the north side of my house will eventually wear out, but I still have to paint it. I can't ignore the white patches. Even if I could, my neighbor can't. He sees them every time he walks from his garage to his house. But I know I have to repaint the side of my house for more than aesthetic reasons. Paint protects and preserves the house itself. My home may be just as temporary as everything else in the physical universe, but I don't want it to be too temporary. I need it to last at least a year or two beyond my thirty-year mortgage.

The Life That Is

This struggle to responsibly maintain material matters is the dilemma we face when we start talking about living for eternity rather than today. Even though I know there is more to life than the appearance of the north side of my house, I still have to take care of the peeling paint. Life is more than clothes and cars and careers, but we still need to cover our bodies. We still need a way of getting around and working to pay for it all. Jesus said life consists of more than food (Luke 12:23), but that doesn't mean we don't have to eat.

However, if we're not careful, we can become so focused on the clothes and cars and food that we can't think of anything else. I know I have to paint the north side of my house, but the act of painting consists of more than going outside with a brush and ladder. I have decisions to make first. Should I go with oil or latex? Flat or satin finish? Perhaps semigloss. And what brand should I buy? After all, I don't want to paint again anytime soon. Which will last longer, the paint with the picture of a little boy in wooden shoes on the label or the one with the profile of a bear just above the name? Perhaps I should go all the way and buy that paint Sears used several years ago to paint Paul Revere's house. Now that's some kind of house paint. At least it looked like it on television. The more I think about it, the more consumed I become with paint, paint, and more PAINT! And I don't even like to paint. If I did, I would have repainted the side of my house last summer.

I'm so sick of thinking about paint that I think I will go to the other extreme. Life is more than paint, so I'm going on a paint-fast for the rest of my life. From this day forward, I will not paint a wall or a porch or even a fingernail. No more paint—that's the only way to find real meaning and lasting happiness.

But the north side of my house still needs to be painted.

The Life That Could Be

The secret to finding meaning and joy in life is not to check out of the real world and go join a monastery somewhere. Vows of poverty, fasting, and silence don't necessarily lead to a well-spent life. They may just leave us poor, hungry, and speechless.

Rather than become a monk (or really depressed), I have to look beyond the daily grind to find what I am looking for. Painting houses and paying bills will always be a part of my existence, but they don't have to define who I am. Living for eternity while dwelling in the world of time means living for something that lasts longer than the paint on my house—something that lives longer than I do. I don't need to be remembered. After all, most of the billions of people who have graced this earth are now long forgotten. Instead I want the impact of my life to continue. The one thing I really want out of life is to live in such a way that my life has a lasting influence on the lives of the people around me, an influence that will last beyond one generation.

Isn't that what we all want?

It's not that we want to change the world. Some people may want that, but most of us don't. At least I don't. I once thought I could change my own little corner of the world, but with my fortieth birthday shrinking further and further away in the rearview mirror, I realize that's not going to happen. Not that it matters. I don't have to change the world to touch it. And that's what my soul longs to do—to make a positive impact on the world while I'm here, continuing on after I die through other human beings. The old English preacher Charles Spurgeon said: "A good character is the best tombstone. Those who loved you, and were helped by you, will remember you when forget-me-nots are withered. Carve your name on hearts and not marble."

To me, this is the very definition of a life well spent. No life will ever be wasted when its character keeps walking around in the lives of those who were touched by it.

Fingerprints on Our Souls

Most of us want to influence future generations in a positive way. Deep down we know this is the something more we've been looking for. We know it because we've felt the gentle touch of others on our own lives. No one ever achieved anything of consequence on his or her own. Our lives are the products of those who cared enough about us to invest their lives in ours. Public television's Mr. Rogers said: "Anyone who has ever graduated from a college, anyone who has ever been able to sustain a good work, has had at least one person and often many who have believed in him or her. We just don't get to be competent human beings without a lot of different investments from others."

Those who invest themselves in our lives do more than inspire us; their impact goes much deeper, affecting the way we see the world and our role in it. They don't touch only our daily existence; their fingerprints are on our souls. Ray Bradbury said it best through his character Granger in *Fahrenheit 451:* "Grandfather's been dead for all these years, but if you lifted my skull, . . . in the convolutions of my brain you'd find the big ridges of his thumbprint. He touched me."[1] If you pried my skull open, you'd find the same kind of thumbprints left behind by people in my life. I'm no self-made man. None of us is. I am who I am because of those who cared enough about me to touch my soul.

But that's only one small part of the picture.

If I could go back in time and pry open the skulls of those who touched my life, I would find the thumbprints of those who loved them enough to do the same. The same would be true of the next generation back, and the next, and the next. The names and the details about their lives are long forgotten, but their influence lives on. Educator and historian Henry Adams once said, "A teacher affects eternity; he can never tell where his influence stops"—a statement that holds true for teachers and nonteachers alike. When one life touches another, it can potentially start a domino effect that will not end. We become, in essence, immortal even after our memory has faded away, through the impact our lives make on the lives of others.

What Is Important?

All this sounds great and wonderful and the very thing you expect from an inspirational book. To think, *I can touch and change generations.* Wow. Maybe I should go find a mountaintop to yell on. *My life may change the lives of those whose parents aren't even born.* Woo-hoo. Praise the Lord. Hallelujah. Amen. Where do I sign up? I'm ready to get started making a positive impact on those around me.

But first . . . I have to paint the north side of my house. Then there's a pile of bills in a drawer that I just have to get to. Boy, this whole business of changing lives for generations sounds like just the thing I've been looking for, but the Yankees play tonight, the first of four crucial games against the evil Red Sox. And the Colts play tomorrow afternoon, which means the weekend is almost over and then it's back to work.

I really plan to jump right on that influence thing, but this is a really crucial time in my business. I'll probably end up working a few nights this week, maybe even through next weekend. It can't be helped. Business is business and you have to pounce on every opportunity, because you just never know when another may present itself. That whole "influence" idea sounds good, but now is not a convenient time. I wouldn't put it off, but these other things are so important they can't be delayed. After all, this is the real world we're talking about.

However, as we saw in the last chapter, the real world isn't as real as we tell ourselves. Sure, there will always be walls that need paint and bills to pay and games to watch. We will always feel the pressure of trying to make a living and to keep business on track. Some days life on this earth feels like a nonstop merry-go-round of expending all of our time and energy just to pay bills that come right back the next month. After awhile we start to define success by our ability to make the merry-go-round work in our favor. We work. We accumulate. We expend all our time and energy on things that don't last, all the while telling ourselves we want something more out of life.

If the one thing we really want out of life is to make a positive impact on generations to come, we need to rearrange our lives to make this goal a reality. This must become both our definition of success and the driving force in our own lives as well. Otherwise, we end up like the guy at work who is always talking about his vacation home in the hills of Kentucky overlooking Lake Cumberland. All day every day this guy goes on and on about his beautiful house in the hills and how he plans to retire there someday. He wants nothing more than to break out of the nine-to-five world and spend the rest of his life in his own personal paradise. Then you go visit this guy's dream home and discover the place is a mess. Weeds nearly obscure the house, the door is hanging off its hinges, half of the windows are broken, and holes cover the roof. The guy's dream home looks like it should be condemned. Although he talks and talks about how much he loves his little house in the hills, one look at it and you can tell the place suffers from neglect.

Talking about devoting ourselves to that which lasts longer than our short lives is nothing but noise if our actions do not follow our words. Each one of us needs to decide what we really want out of life. We need to figure out what it will take for us to call this brief existence time well spent. Then we need to pursue this with nothing held back. Words are easy. Now is the time for action.

Where to Begin?

The ability to touch and change future generations sounds like such a noble quest, but we should understand that we are already influencing those closest to us in some way without any special effort on our part. We rub off on others just as they rub off on us simply from hanging around one another. Unconvinced? Try spending some time with someone with a thick accent. In no time at all, their speech patterns will imprint themselves on your tongue. Before you know it, you'll find yourself saying "y'all" or "yous guys" and calling sodas "pop" or pop "sodas," or if you spend any time with someone from Oklahoma, you'll call every carbonated beverage "Coke," even when ordering a Dr Pepper. The Bible says bad company corrupts good morals (1 Cor. 15:33), because all of us tend to act like whomever we're around. And since we spend more time with family than anyone else (at least during our formative years), certain tendencies and character qualities, both good and bad, are passed down within families from generation to generation. We may live on through the habits we pass down to our children and grandchildren, but the habits may be useless. If my grandchildren someday love the New York Yankees, I can't say my time on earth was worth the effort.

To again quote Mr. Fred Rogers: "If only you could sense how important you are to the lives of those you meet; how important you can be to people you may never even dream of. There is something of yourself that you leave at every meeting with another person."

If I'm going to leave something of myself with every person I meet, I want to make sure I leave the right something, which takes us back to the last chapter's ending: influence begins with humility. As long as I remain large in my own eyes, I will never sense the importance of other people, because I can't see them. My own self blocks my view. I'm too busy staring at myself. My needs. My wants. My plans. That's all that matters to me. But when I put on humility, I fade from view, setting myself free to become a servant. Then my life can touch and change those whom God brings into my life. Only then will my life matter.

Why humility? Can't I inspire those around me without downsizing my view of myself? Frankly, no. You already know nothing on this earth lasts. Eventually everything comes to an end and is forgotten. This is where smallness and humility come in. The Bible promises that anything we do during our lifetimes for God will last throughout eternity. The smallest act—something as inconsequential as giving a glass of cold water to someone who is thirsty—matters when it is done for God (Mark 9:41). I can't help but be struck by the irony in all this. People spend their entire lives making a name for themselves. They'll make any sacrifice or pay any price to build a business or win a gold medal or fulfill a childhood dream. But once they are gone, that's it. Their life's work doesn't mean a thing on an eternal scale.

However, the smallest, simplest, most overlooked tasks any Tom, Dick, or Mary can do, when done for the sake of Jesus Christ, make an impact that cannot be confined by time. The only size that matters when it comes to tasks done for God is the size of our God. He can do amazing things with the smallest of materials. In the New Testament Jesus took a handful of fish and a couple of loaves of bread and fed five thousand people with them. Just imagine what He can do with your life and mine when we put them in His hands. This is the place where purpose and joy come together and fill our lives. In his classic work *No Little People*, Francis Schaeffer put it this way as he compared the way God can use our lives with the way He used Moses' shepherd rod: "Those who think of themselves as little people in little places, if committed to Christ and living under His lordship in the whole of life, may, by God's grace, change the flow of our generation. And as we get on a bit in our lives, knowing how weak we are, if we look back and see we have been somewhat used by God, then we should be the rod 'surprised by joy.'"[2]

Isn't that what we want out of life?

Chapter 3

Visions of Grandeur

The proper time to influence the character of a
child is about a hundred years before he is born.

W. R. INGE

▪▪

[God] established a testimony in Jacob and set up
a law in Israel, which He commanded our fathers
to teach to their children so that a future generation—
children yet to be born—might know. They were
to rise and tell their children.

PSALM 78:5–6

*E*d had a dream for his six children: he wanted them all
to go to college. The dream doesn't seem so remarkable
until you consider Ed and his wife, Pearl, had their children
before the days of Pell Grants and Sallie Mae school loans.
Nor did Ed and Pearl have much money. Few people trying
to scratch out a living in farming the southwest corner of
Oklahoma in the 1920s and '30s did.

I'm not sure when Ed's dream was born, but it may have
been during the extended drought known as the Dust Bowl.
The name came from the clouds of red and black dust that
covered the Texas panhandle and western Oklahoma. Each

day the wind kicked up and the dust flew. It seeped through every crack and crevice of Ed and Pearl's small farmhouse. Despite all her efforts, Pearl couldn't keep it out, but that didn't stop her from trying. Each day she and the dust joined in a bizarre waltz. Pearl swept it out the door, only to watch the dust dance right back inside.

Many farmers gave up the fight and headed toward California. Steinbeck wrote about them in *The Grapes of Wrath*. Many years later, Ed and Pearl's grandchildren joked about how the family had been too poor to leave their farm to go west. Instead they stayed, fighting the dust and trying to coax wheat, peanuts, and cotton to pop up out of the red dirt without the aid of rain.

Maybe that's why Ed wanted his three sons and three daughters to go to college. He'd never gone himself. His education consisted of a few years in a one-room schoolhouse in east Texas. When he came of age, Ed went looking for a place where he could make a life of his own. He ended up on a plot of ground that was a part of Oklahoma only because the Red River took a sharp turn south directly before it reached his farm. There he met Pearl. Soon afterward, the two married and started a family. Like any father, he wanted to give his children a better life than his own. He wanted to set them free from watching cotton plants shrivel and die, while gaping cracks formed in the fields under an August sun. In his eyes, a college education was their only ticket to freedom.

Ed and Pearl's oldest daughter never made it to college. Like her mother, she fell in love with a dirt farmer and married at a young age. But her sisters went off to school along with all three of her brothers. Each went to the same school, Oklahoma Agricultural and Mechanical College, but then, where else would a farmer's children go? Shortly after the youngest finished, the state changed the name to Oklahoma State University. One of Ed's sons went on to become a lawyer, another became a pastor, and the third was a schoolteacher before going into business. One daughter became a teacher. The other sister dropped out to get married, but she passed Ed's dream on to her children. All his children did.

I've been thinking about Ed a lot the past few days. I'll probably think about him even more as my wife and I prepare to send another daughter off to college in a few weeks. Ed is partly responsible for her going—with his dream for his six children. My daughters are just the latest chapter in a story that continues to unfold. The man with a dream died before my father met my mother, which meant I would never know my paternal grandfather. Even so, his dream changed my life, and now it's changing the lives of my children as well.

Definition of Success

My grandfather never had much. He didn't leave behind the kind of inheritance people go to court to fight over, nor does anything bearing his name still stand in or around Altus, Oklahoma. You won't find a statue in his honor in the town square. Even his burial plot has been forgotten by everyone except a handful of people. Yet the impact of his life lives on. I don't know if Ed ever sat down and thought about his great grandchildren or his great-great grandchildren. He simply had a dream for the six kids bouncing around his small farmhouse in a dusty corner of Oklahoma. Today his descendants include doctors, lawyers, college professors, military officers, ministers, and writers, just to name a few. The man who never had much—a nobody from nowhere— lived a life that defines lasting success.

Stories like Ed's are all around us. The people who influence generations aren't the giants of history, but the easy-to-ignore plain and ordinary men and women who invested their lives in the lives of others. They are the real American success stories, fulfilling the true American dream. Greatness can't be measured in terms of stock options or the square footage of a house. True success comes through the small acts that make a lifetime of difference in one generation after another. The question then becomes, *How can I make my life successful?*

It all starts with character.

Before any of us can touch and influence generations, we need to have a life worth passing down. Pardon my bluntness, but the world has enough self-centered, ego-driven, spoiled-rotten moral relativists who think the entire universe revolves around them. We don't need any more.

The world needs men and women of character who embody integrity, honor, sacrifice, humility, and loyalty. I guess I should insert a line or two about how character worth passing down to other generations begins with a personal relationship with Jesus Christ. It does, but the link isn't automatic. If you live with the mistaken notion that God exists to make you happy, your life needs to undergo a dramatic overhaul before you will taste any sort of real success. Jesus said, "If anyone wants to be My follower, he must deny himself, take up his cross, and follow Me. For whoever wants to save his life will lose it, but whoever loses his life because of Me and the gospel will save it" (Mark 8:34–35).

Finding a life worth living begins with living in the eternal even while stuck in the temporal, and character starts with surrendering my life to the God who lives outside of time. My life isn't about me, and as long as I live as though

27

it is, I don't have anything to pass on to the next generation. However, once I deny myself, take up my cross, and start following Jesus, He is able to reproduce His character in me—character that I can then begin to instill into the lives of others. The apostle Paul once said, "Be imitators of me, as I also am of Christ" (1 Cor. 11:1). That's the idea here. Imitating Christ will make a dramatic change in three specific areas of your life, changes worth passing along to others.

1. Values

When we move from the temporal world to the eternal worlds, the things that are important to us move as well. In the world of time, we worry a lot about food and clothes and career. But when we move to the realm of the eternal, we will "seek first the kingdom of God and His righteousness" (Matt. 6:33), and leave the rest to God. His plan and His will become our first priority. Jesus said all the commands in the Bible boil down to these two: love God and love people (see Mark 12:29–31). In a nutshell, these are the values God places in our lives. People mean more than power, prestige, or possessions, and God means more than anything else.

Whatever is most important to you sets the agenda for everything else you do in your life. What we say matters most to us is really irrelevant. Our checkbooks and our schedules give the real answer. The difficult questions each one of us must ask ourselves is, *Are my values really valuable and are they worth passing along to others?*

2. Integrity

God doesn't change and He cannot lie. His character is always consistent with His Word. He always keeps His promises even when doing so causes Him pain. Never once has He reneged on a contract He made with human beings. Some people think He is distant and hard to please, but that's because they don't know Him very well. Both the Bible and history reveal Him as loving and eager to forgive. Above all, He is holy and just. People scream at Him and accuse Him of being unfair, but the charges don't stick. Even though we don't see it now, a day is coming when God will set everything right, and those who oppressed the poor and the powerless will get what is coming to them. The righteous God will see to it. He stands up for justice even while offering His grace to those who will turn to Him.

God embodies integrity. His goal for you and me is to make us like Himself. Living for eternity means opening up our lives to Him and letting Him have His way with us. Slowly but surely He chips away at everything that doesn't belong in our lives, everything that mars the family resemblance He wants to stamp on His children. A life of integrity means letting Him do just that. As long as we fight Him, we have nothing to pass on to anyone else.

3. Passion

God is passionate about you and me. He longs to draw us close to Him, and will pay any price to make that happen. In fact, He already has. God's Son, Jesus, died on a cross to remove the offense of our sins so that we could be forgiven and adopted into God's family. That's not just love. That's passion.

Passionate people rub off on those around them. Years ago we lived in California. When we arrived I thought there were only two sports in the entire world: baseball and football. But then I was introduced to the Los Angeles Lakers by a friend named Dan. Before he moved to our small mountain community, Dan lived next door to Kurt Rambis, then a reserve forward for the Lakers. It didn't take long for Dan's passion for the Lakers to rub off on me, and for me to rub off on my wife. We would yell and scream at the television as Magic Johnson, Kareem Abdul Jabbar, Byron Scott, James Worthy, and A. C. Green sprinted down the court in a fast break. My wife even took me to the Great Western Forum to watch the Lakers in person for my thirtieth birthday.

When you spend time with God, His passion rubs off on you as well. The more time we spend with Him, the more passionate we will become about righteousness and justice and holiness, but especially about people. Like God, we will get very passionate about seeing people coming to know the God who gave up His Son for them. As God rubs off on us, He wants us to rub off on others. Successful living begins with godly character. Until we have it, we won't have anything to give to anyone else.

Character is the prerequisite for a successful life that changes generations. Without it, you might as well stop reading now. It's like going to the grocery store without any money. You can spend all day in there wandering around in the aisles, but you still leave with nothing.

Now don't get me wrong. I'm not saying that if you aren't perfect you need to go hide in the Himalayas to keep from infecting anyone else with your bad habits. We all are, after all, still human. The aftereffects of the Fall will be with us until the day we die. None of us will ever be perfect. Even the apostle Paul, a man who wrote thirteen books of the New Testament, considered himself a work in progress. He wrote, "I'm not saying that I have this all together, that I have it made. But I am well on my way, reaching out for Christ, who has so wondrously reached out for me" (Phil. 3:12 MSG).

The mark of character isn't perfection, but the unwavering pursuit to see more of God's handiwork in our lives each day. With that as our goal, we are ready to start working toward lasting success. To do that we must then get close enough to others to make a difference in their lives.

Proximity

The key to a successful life—a life that impacts lives today and generations to come—isn't exactly rocket science. Or maybe it is, since rocket science isn't as complicated as I once thought . . . at least that's the impression my friend the rocket scientist gave me. He told me the basics of rocket science go back to the simple thrust principles formulated by a mathematician named Heron who lived in Alexandria more than 2,200 years ago. Heron demonstrated the first simple reaction engine (basically, a sphere that rotated when small opposing nozzles spouted steam onto it). Small, simple rockets, like those my dad and I used to set off in our backyard on the Fourth of July, have been around for a thousand years.

In 1926, Robert Goddard built and launched the first liquid-fueled rocket, the forerunner of the rocket that later took Neil Armstrong, Buzz Aldrin, and Michael Collins to the moon and back. The designs have advanced through the years, along with the materials used to build rockets, but the basic science hasn't. The secrets were discovered a long, long time ago.

In the same way, the secrets of true success have been around a long time. It starts with character, but it doesn't stop there. We will find true success as we . . . here it comes, the big secret, I can hardly contain my excitement . . . success comes as we . . . I can tell you, this is going to be really,

really profound . . . successful living, a life that is well spent means . . . drum roll, please . . . building relationships with people and spending quality time with them, through which the character God has developed inside of you rubs off on those around you.

It all comes down to proximity.

The greatest influencer the world has ever known used this approach. Jesus came to earth with a mission. His Father sent Him here to save the world. During the short time He spent on the earth, He launched a movement intended to reach every corner of the globe. Jesus had one distinct advantage for making His mission a success: He was God in human flesh, the second Person of the Trinity, the One through whom the entire universe was created in six days. Needless to say, He possessed the power to rock the world.

But Jesus didn't put on a show to amaze the masses. Although He performed miracles, He never did anything that would force the entire world to turn to Him. Most of the time, He did just the opposite. Whenever the crowds grew too large, He moved to another part of the country where He wasn't known.

All the while He did something rather strange for the Savior of the world intent on causing global change: instead of drumming up support among the masses, Jesus invested the three short years of His earthly ministry into a group of ordinary men who lacked both the influence and the access to get things done. They were just a bunch of fisherman and ex-tax collectors and overall ordinary people. Yet these were the men Jesus spent all of His time with. He poured Himself into this small group of twelve. This was God Incarnate's brilliant plan for changing the entire course of history.

And it worked.

Jesus' life shows that the character that changes generations isn't so much taught as caught. You can't just corner
some poor soul on an airplane and spend the entire flight
from Newark to Los Angeles enlightening him with your
collected wisdom. Influence must be caught as it is passed
from one life to another over time. It can't be distributed to
large crowds all at once like a flu vaccine. That's not to say
people like Billy Graham who speak to tens of thousands at
a time don't affect our behavior. They can and do. But as I
look back over my life, I find the impact the big names have
made on me is much smaller than the obscure folks in the
crowd who invested their lives into mine.

C. S. Lewis, my favorite author, has profoundly changed
my understanding of God. Yet, for all I've learned from his
books, his influence has been far less than Boyd Rayburn,
the pastor of the small suburban church I grew up in. No
one ever put Boyd on the radio or his sermons into books
for the masses to enjoy. To be honest, I can't remember anything he ever said from the pulpit, but that's not where his
life touched mine. His youngest son and I were best friends
growing up. Through the years, I ate a lot of meals in his
home and spent time with Boyd and his family in a variety
of settings. He showed me close up what it meant to serve
God on a daily basis and implanted in me the desire to do
the same.

You can't impact lives at a distance or in haste. Real
influence takes time. Lots and lots of time. And this isn't
the kind of time you can simply schedule into your day. The
best teaching moments aren't even teaching moments at all.
Jesus rubbed off on His disciples as they walked around the
countryside of Galilee, Samaria, and Judea. They listened
as He taught the crowds, but His biggest impact occurred

Chapter 4

Don't Make Me Be Last

Most of us know we will never be the greatest;
just don't let us be the least.
RICHARD FOSTER, *CELEBRATION OF DISCIPLINE*

▬▬▬▬▬▬▬▬▬▬▬▬▬▬▬▬

He must increase, but I must decrease.
JOHN THE BAPTIST, JOHN 3:30

*H*e knows he can get anyone in the family to do whatever he wants, and he uses this power frequently. Although he is just a year old and weighs less than ten pounds, he manipulates human beings like pawns in his own little game of chess. No one can tell him no. When they try to, he turns on the charm and they melt in his paws. He doesn't care about schedules or how busy anyone in the household might be, not when he wants his belly rubbed. Whenever he spies a potential belly-rubber, he quickly rolls over on his very long back, pulls his front feet up to his chest, and flashes a "come hither" look. Someone always complies. The same holds true when he wants to play fetch or when he needs a warm body to snuggle up against on a cold Indiana morning. No one can resist the charm of a miniature dachshund puppy, at least not one as cute and cuddly as this little guy. And he knows it.

The newest member of our family is a canine of influence. Many people would like to know the secret of his success . . . make that all people. Who wouldn't want to have the magic touch to get people to do whatever we want whenever we want? And there are plenty of voices out there telling us how to do it. I recently came across a book that promises to teach me to

get the instant advantage in any relationship
get anyone to take my advice
get a stubborn person to change his mind about anything
get anyone to do a favor for me
get anyone to return my phone call
stop verbal abuse instantly.[1]

Wow! Now that's what I call influence. In the first chapter I asked what we really want out of life. When it comes to the here and now, the above list pretty much sums it up for most of us. Possessing the power to get people to do what I want when I want, and then making them think it was their idea all along sounds like the ticket to a happy life. That explains why books like this are so popular. We flock to them not because we're self-centered creatures intent on manipulating other people to get our way. Our motives are much more noble. We just want to make that sale or get that promotion or advance our careers. We just want to be happy, and that desire for happiness gets in the way of making our lives count.

The 800-Pound Gorilla

We all want to be happy. Explaining why is like trying to explain why we prefer chicken Parmesan or meatloaf and mashed potatoes to dry bread crusts and water. We just do. It's what makes us human. We long to be happy and most of us will do whatever it takes to be so. We measure success in life by how happy we feel at any given time. Yet the desire for happiness goes beyond smiles and laughter. Deep down we long for a settled state of happiness, a "happily ever after" that doesn't fade away with time. We hope this state lurks out there somewhere as the holy grail of living.

If we have to spend our entire lives searching for it, we won't mind, just as long as we finally find it. That's why people use the phrase "I knew this was my one shot at happiness" to justify any action, and no one argues the point. The quest for happiness has become the highest good, the 800-pound gorilla of life that shoves everything else out of its way.

Letting this gorilla run our lives will never lead us to a life that matters. Elevating my happiness above everything else causes my whole world to become about me, myself, and I. My wants. My needs. My desires. Me, me, me, and more me. I would be lying if I said this path led to an unhappy life, because it doesn't. Self-centered people can be the happiest people in the world, especially if they have the means to indulge all their desires. Yet at the end of their lives, what exactly have they accomplished?

This doesn't mean that selfish people can't change the world and influence generations to come. They can and do. In fact, the most successful people in this world can be among the most arrogant and self-absorbed. They conquer nations, build empires, and make it impossible for the rest of the world to ignore them. We can't ignore them because they blast us with noise about themselves.

37

Watching the rich and powerful become more rich and powerful is like watching a little kid with a big purple crayon write his name on everything he sees. Everyone knows who he is because his name is everywhere.

Self-centered people also wield influence that lasts. They change the way we do business, alter the forms of entertainment we enjoy, and imprint their worldview on the culture as a whole. Yet the ability to shape culture doesn't automatically translate into a well-spent life, nor does it set generations free from the tyranny of the temporary to live for eternity.

There is a better way.

An Upside-down World

Jesus made some very strange statements about happiness. Just listen to a few: "Those people who know they have great spiritual needs are happy, because the kingdom of heaven belongs to them. Those who are sad now are happy, because God will comfort them. Those who are humble are happy, because the earth will belong to them" (Matt. 5:3–5 NCV).

As if those aren't strange enough, He topped them all with this: "Those who are treated badly for doing good are happy, because the kingdom of heaven belongs to them. People will insult you and hurt you. They will lie and say all kinds of evil things about you because you follow me. But when they do, you will be happy. Rejoice and be glad, because you have a great reward waiting for you in heaven. People did the same evil things to the prophets who lived before you" (Matt. 5:10–12 NCV).

All I can say is, *What?!* Most translations use the word blessed instead of "happy" in these verses, which removes some of the weirdness. However, when Jesus first spoke these lines, He used a word that means "happy." In fact, the word implies these sad, persecuted, humble people are not just happy, but very happy. They are "privileged recipients of divine favor."[2] That means God has given them His very best.

Sandwiched in between the above statements, Jesus uttered a few more, all of which describe the path to happiness in terms of putting others in front of yourself. Jesus seems to be saying that if we want to find true, lasting happiness and to enter the blessed life in which God's best rains down on us, we need to ignore conventional wisdom and do just the opposite of what our natural instincts tell us to do. He turns the world upside down by saying eternal happiness can't be found in self-indulgence but through self-sacrifice.

Having all of my needs met won't bring me the happiness my soul desires. I find something far greater when I allow God to work through me to meet the needs of others. By doing so, I become God's conduit for justice, mercy, and peace to those who desperately need it (Matt. 5:6–7, 9). In the process I find something better than happiness: I discover the joy that comes from becoming a servant.

Jesus didn't just spout these words. He lived them. To see how, you must understand that Jesus wasn't just some guy who lived a long time ago in a far-away place whose life grew to mythical proportions. Before coming to earth, Jesus sat on heaven's throne. He was, and is, fully God, the second Person of the Trinity. Everything that exists—from microscopic bits of matter to the largest galaxies in the universe— came into being because He told it to. He spoke and the physical universe sprang into existence. Since He made it, He also owns it, and according to Colossians 1:17, He is also holding everything together. Apart from Jesus, the entire physical universe would cease to exist. This is who Jesus is and who He has always been.

The Creator then became a part of the physical universe by becoming a man. Don't worry if your mind has trouble wrapping itself around that sentence. I don't understand how matter can be all fuzzy and foamy on a quantum level and still be solid. That doesn't make much sense to me, but my lack of understanding doesn't change the fact that it is true. In the same way, I don't completely understand exactly how God could take on human flesh and come to earth as a human being while remaining God. But the Bible says He did and His name was Jesus.

The second chapter of Paul's letter to the church in Philippi says that even though Jesus was God, He didn't use His equality with God the Father to His own advantage (Phil. 2:6). Instead He left the glories of heaven to be born in a barn to poor parents in an insignificant country. I can't come up with an analogy to what Jesus did. If Donald Trump left his New York penthouse and moved into a cardboard shack in the slums of San Paulo, Brazil, it still wouldn't compare.

Not only did God take on human flesh, He assumed the form of a servant (Phil. 2:7). Jesus Himself said, "The Son of Man did not come to be served, but to serve, and to give His life—a ransom for many" (Matt. 20:28). His ultimate act of service came when He allowed Himself to be nailed to a cross to die like any ordinary criminal for you and me. Why would He do such a thing? Hebrews 12:2 says He endured the shame of the cross "for the joy that lay before Him."

Now when we hear Jesus tell us to downsize our lives and start serving other people, we can't dismiss His words as nothing more than religious jargon. He doesn't just tell us what to do; He shows us. You and I must downsize our lives to make them small enough to matter, just as Jesus did. The path to everlasting joy, the road to everything our souls long for, leads us down the path of being a servant. There is no other way. The key isn't just serving others. Choosing to serve doesn't make my life small enough. I have to become a servant. Richard Foster put it this way: "When we choose to serve, we are still in charge. We decide whom we will serve and when we will serve. And if we are in charge, we will worry a great deal about anyone's stepping on us, that is, taking charge over us. But when we choose to be a servant, we give up the right to be in charge. . . . We become available and vulnerable."[3]

What, then, do I have to do to become a servant?

Make Me a Servant

Just because I wrote this doesn't mean that all of this humility and service come naturally to me. I struggle with servanthood as much as anyone. To be honest, I'm struggling to write this. The first few chapters of this book have proven to be the hardest thing I've ever written. I couldn't wait to actually put down on paper these thoughts that were running around in my head, but every day at my keyboard has been a cage fight between this book and me.

Why? Downsizing myself in my daily life is hard. I can do the "aw shucks" fake humility all day long. You know the kind—someone pays you a compliment and you try to deflect it with a couple of "aw shucks, it weren't nothings." That's not humility. Nor is humility constantly putting yourself down and thinking the things you do aren't any good or becoming everyone's doormat because you can't say no to anything. Doing any of those is easy. Real humility, the kind that gives you the heart of a servant, always comes with a struggle. At least it does for me.

Practicing humility, downsizing myself, becoming a servant—each demands I make a conscious choice to submit myself to the will of God. By doing so, I make a conscious decision to consider other people more important than I am. This was what Jesus did when He walked on this earth, and He now calls us to do the same. Both acts, submission to God and serving other people, flow from the previously noted two greatest commandments: "Love the Lord your God with all your heart, with all your soul, and with all your mind. . . . Love your neighbor as yourself" (Matt. 22:37, 39). I express my love to God by obeying Him with a joyful heart, and I show love to other people by putting them ahead of myself.

That's all there is to it. It looks pretty simple, doesn't it? But, of course, we know it isn't, at least not once you actually move from the realm of theory to the real world. Submitting my will to the will of God means obeying Him even when I don't want to, and I often don't want to because some of His commands hurt.

It was easy for me to say yes when He called me to write books about Him, but when He told me to forgive the woman who inflicted a great deal of pain on me and my family, I wasn't so eager to obey. I could mouth the words, "I forgive her," but I still wanted to extract a pound of flesh. Deep down I wanted to see her paid back for everything she'd done. Five years later part of me still wants a little revenge. God keeps telling me to let it go, and I think that I have . . . until I bump into her at the grocery store. Then, when anger flashes in my mind, I suddenly realize my will isn't quite as bent toward God as I'd thought.

Considering others to be more important than I am is also easy—in theory. I can sit in church and look around at the people in the room and think warm thoughts toward them all day long. That little fake, church smile crosses my lips as I think, "Yes, I *will* put all of these people before myself." Church ends and I drive up the street with my family to the local Cracker Barrel to eat lunch with some friends. The friendly hostess tells us we'll have to wait perhaps ten or fifteen minutes. We put our name on the list and start waiting for a table to become available (even though I would rather go next door to the Mexican restaurant because I'm not that wild about Cracker Barrel). Ten or fifteen minutes go by, and we still don't have a table. However, another family from church who arrived after us gets seated. As I watch them walk into the dining room while I'm stuck in the country store, milling around the DVDs of *Andy Griffith* and *The Beverly Hillbillies,* my first thought is, *That's not fair! I was here first!* Then it hits me: all my talk about putting others first didn't even last an hour. I mentally ran right back to that little corner of the universe where everything revolves around me.

That's why Jesus tells us to choose the smallest place, both in terms of importance but also in size:

"When you are invited by someone to a wed-
ding banquet, don't recline at the best place,
because a more distinguished person than you
may have been invited by your host. The one who
invited both of you may come and say to you,
'Give your place to this man,' and then in humili-
ation, you will proceed to take the lowest place.

43

But when you are invited, go and recline in the
lowest place, so that when the one who invited
you comes, he will say to you, 'Friend, move up
higher.' You will then be honored in the presence
of all the other guests. For everyone who exalts
himself will be humbled, and the one who humbles
himself will be exalted." (Luke 14:8–11)

Choosing the smaller place makes it easier for me to submit my will to the will of God. It also makes it easier for me
to serve other people effectively. We sometimes think that
if we are in a bigger, more prominent place, we will be able
to reach more people and do more for God. But the kingdom of heaven doesn't work that way. God says to choose
the smaller place until He moves us into a larger one. Until
then, our choice must be for the small place, the insignificant
place, where I can lose the battle against myself and serve
others.

Filling Water Glasses

Becoming a servant and impacting generations go hand
in hand. I influence lives by considering others to be more
important than I am and pouring out my life into theirs.
When I get serious about doing this, I realize I need to clear
all the junk out of my life that gets in my way and get my
schedule under control to do what is most important to me.
More than anything, I have to make my life small enough to
matter in the lives of those God has placed around me.

Part of me still wonders why I have to downsize myself
to accomplish anything of eternal significance. After all,
wouldn't my time be better spent if I tried to impact as many
people as I possibly could? Even if I could only make a small

contribution to the life of another, wouldn't a little influence in the lives of thousands or tens of thousands be better than a lot of influence in only a handful of lives? I don't think so. When I go to a restaurant, I don't want the waiter with the most tables to serve. I want the one with the fewest. A waiter trying to take orders from hundreds of customers won't serve me nearly as well as the one with just a handful.

That's the principle here. Life is short. James 4:14 says our entire life spans are little more than the cloud of vapor I see when I exhale on a cold January morning. In a matter of seconds the fog disappears, and no one gives it a second thought. That is exactly what our lives are—a brief fog that quickly vanishes into the morning air. Because life is short, I want mine to count. I want my life to be small enough to matter.

Living out this decision doesn't come easily, not in the real world. Too many things get in our way and crowd out what matters most to us. If we do not take firm action, all of our good intentions will be buried under a pile of bills and activities. Making my life smaller begins by downsizing myself, putting on humility, and becoming a servant.

But that's only the beginning. To make these priorities stick, to make them a permanent part of my life, I also need to downsize every other aspect of my life, especially my material possessions and my schedule. My life needs to become not only smaller but simpler and saner. That means clearing out the clutter and the chaos. Only then will my life be in a position to touch and change generations.

Simpler

Chapter 5
Forfeited Souls

So many people walk around with a
meaningless life. They seem half-asleep, even when
they're busy doing things they think are important.
This is because they're chasing the wrong things.
MITCH ALBOM, *TUESDAYS WITH MORRIE*

‖‖‖

For what does it benefit a man to gain
the whole world yet lose his life?
MARK 8:36

*I*n every life, stuff accumulates. It fills your attics, garages,
closets, and every available square inch of space. You don't
mean to hoard, but six little words keep spinning around
in your head: It might be worth something someday. The
words stop you from throwing anything out. And so it piles
up—commemorative Wheaties boxes featuring the 1998
Women's Olympic Hockey Team and the 1991 Minnesota
Twins, ticket stubs from a 1971 Elvis concert, and an eight-
by-ten glossy of Robert Goulet. There's a World Series program you ordered by mail and a miniature batting helmet
that doubled as a sundae dish from the Cincinnati Reds 2000
home opener, both sitting atop boxes of Superman comics

and *Mad* magazines. It would be nice to be able to pull the car into the garage, but that would mean exposing the 1978 AMC Pacer to snow and rain and summer sun, and you can't do that because it might be worth something someday.

You consider cleaning it all out, hauling the Bill and Monica newspapers to the recycling bin and giving the Princess Di Beanie Babies and *NSYNC bobblehead dolls to underprivileged kids at Christmas, but the six words make you put up extra shelves. You carefully wrap the *E.T.* cereal cards in plastic and place the *Beauty and the Beast* Happy Meal toys in Tupperware. The last car you owned with an eight-track tape player gave up the ghost two decades ago, but you keep holding on to *Foghat Live* and *Hotel California* and Willie Nelson's *Redheaded Stranger.* They don't take up much space, and besides, they might be worth something someday.

A man on *Antiques Roadshow* turned an old sword into instant cash, which makes your Luke Skywalker lightsaber an investment in your children's future. And the G. I. Joe Jeep and the Barbie Winnebago will surely catch someone's eye on eBay. Who knows what a collector will pay for the 3-D Joe Morgan baseball card you dug out of a box of cornflakes when you were ten or that 1981 Sears catalog in mint condition. But you can't part with them yet, not while their value is climbing. After all, they might be worth something someday.

To whom, you don't know, and how much is anyone's guess, but the day will surely come when your diligent collecting and innocent hoarding will be rewarded. Then the chorus of voices that chided you for never throwing anything out will eat their words. Your house is cluttered and your garage is filled and the attic sags under the weight of stuff, but none of that will matter then. You had the fore-sight, you had the vision, you had the wisdom to know that it might be worth something someday.

An Insecure World

While you wait for its value to climb, that stuff gets in your way of living a life that matters. The root problem isn't just an insatiable desire for more. You can curb greed and still have day-to-day necessities get in your way of real life. Nor is contentment the sole answer. The Bible tells us to be satisfied with whatever we have (Heb. 13:5), yet learning to master this discipline alone will not clear stuff out of your way. We hold onto stuff and accumulate more and more in part because we long for something that cannot be found in this temporal world. We're looking for security, but we will never find it in this insecure world. No one knows what tomorrow may hold. The same future that may cause our collection of vintage Star Wars action figures to skyrocket in value may just as easily bring financial disaster.

The longing for security gets in the way of our pursuit of a life that matters, a life that impacts lives for generations. The process is gradual. It sucks us in so slowly, so effort-lessly, that we don't even realize what is happening. The process begins with a mild case of amnesia. (I can't think of another term to describe the way we forget that nothing in this world is certain.) The amnesia sets in and we start act-ing like we can know tomorrow. We buy. We sell. We make big plans. We incur debts, both big and small. We live a per-fectly normal life—in the eyes of the temporal world. But the uncertainty of living in a world where no one knows what tomorrow may hold cannot be ignored forever. Before long, the truth shoves itself into our faces and a strange sensation sweeps over us. It starts with a funny feeling in the pit of our stomachs and then grows like a hurricane passing over tropical waters. Before we know it, a full-scale case of worry has us in its grip.

Remember, the first step toward finding the life we crave is to step out of the world of time and into the eternal realm where God dwells. Worry does just the opposite. It is, at its heart, the natural response of a life completely oriented toward the temporal. Regardless of what we say we believe about God, when we worry, we live as though the physical universe is all there is, or at least, all that matters. And if this world is all there is, we should worry. A lot. In fact, if this world is all there is, we might as well skip right past worry and move right on to panic, because the future doesn't look bright at all. And those thoughts of an uncertain future are what got this process going in the first place.

Insecurity breeds worry. It launches all sorts of thoughts with words like "how" and "what if" and "might" and "maybe" and "oh my!" You know the thoughts. They've run through your head just like they've run through mine. With two kids in college and another headed there in a couple of years, thoughts like these visit me almost every day if I leave the door open to them. But worry is just one part of the equation. We can't continue to live in a state of constant anxiety. Perhaps we could, but I, for one, can't afford that much Maalox. Eventually we have to do something about it.

More and More

Fueled by worry, insecurity then drives us to acquire and hoard. Money and the things it can buy become our source of security. The apostle Paul once said if he had food and clothing, he would be content with that (1 Tim. 6:8). Most of us need a little more to feel really safe. A good job, an expanding savings account, a solid IRA, employer-matching pension funds—they all make us feel better about the future and allow us to stop popping Tums and enjoy life.

We can say God is our only hope, but who among us doesn't sleep better at night when the bills are all paid and there's still money left in the bank? I'll admit I do. Yet the world never stops its relentless lurch into the unknown, which means we can never feel completely at ease with what we have. Life keeps getting more expensive even as we realize that no job situation is secure. To stay ahead, we have to keep on accumulating to prepare for any eventuality.

Don't get me wrong. I know there are things we need to live in this world. God knows this as well. His Word tells us He knows what we need even before we do (Matt. 6:8). However, the more we focus on those daily needs, the fuzzier the real reason for our existence becomes. Stuff fills our field of vision until we can't see anything else. We not only use possessions as our source of security, we also begin to use them as a gauge for worth. We judge ourselves and others by the volume of our possessions, which fuels the desire for more. The more we own, the more we must have.

After awhile the desire for security gives way to the longing for comfort, although our vocabulary remains the same. The word *want* is replaced by the word *need,* as in I *need* a bigger house or I *need* a better car or I *need* a more powerful computer even though I rarely do anything more than write letters, send e-mail, and play solitaire on the one I have. Again, the real problem isn't the house or the car or the computer, but in the orientation of our lives. First Corinthians 7:31 says this world in its present form is passing away, but we act as though it is going to last forever. When our lives are lived in the world of time rather than the eternal, we will never see material stuff in the proper light. Our craving for security gives way to a longing for comfort, which in turn leaves us believing that more stuff will make us happier than we are today.

The worst possible thing we can do is to bring God into the mix without shifting our focal point away from the temporal. When we do, we end up turning Him into a celestial ATM that exists to give us the things we need in this world to make us feel safe, secure, and above all, happy. As a result we start misreading the Bible and misapplying God's promises.

Ephesians 1:3 tells us God has blessed those who follow His Son with every spiritual blessing in the heavenly realm. When our entire lives are oriented toward the physical world, we think this verse means God will make us wealthy with material possessions, even though it says nothing of the kind. The blessings God gives us in His Son can never be confined to something so temporary.

Jesus said, "Foxes have dens and birds of the sky have nests, but the Son of Man has no place to lay His head" (Matt. 8:20), which means the Savior of the world was homeless; yet that doesn't stop some from claiming God wants to give His children palatial homes in this world. Even without going to such extremes we can still turn God into nothing more than a blessing machine. If we are completely honest, don't most of us assume that if we follow Jesus by faith, God will make our lives (and physical comforts) on this earth better?

Forfeited Souls

Jesus said, "And how do you benefit if you gain the whole world but lose your own soul in the process?" (Mark 8:36 NLT). If we have already committed our lives to Jesus Christ, we may assume these words no longer apply to us, but they do. When we spend our lives working toward financial security, when all of our time and energy goes into carving out better lives for ourselves and our children (even though we aren't trying to get rich; we're just trying to get ahead and put a little space between ourselves and the bill collectors), at the end of our lives we will look back and see we lost what really mattered.

The quest for financial security will never take us where we want to go in life, because we end up chasing something that doesn't exist. Solomon said it best, "Enjoy prosperity while you can. But when hard times strike, realize that both come from God. That way you will realize that *nothing is certain in this life*" (Eccles. 7:14 NLT, italics added). When we live as though material possessions will give us a sense of certainty, we end up forfeiting our souls. Our time on earth is wasted and we never come close to living the life God had planned for us.

Jesus told a story about a farmer who, one season, had the harvest to end all harvests. His fields produced beyond his wildest dreams. So much grain flowed into his barns that they couldn't hold it all, so the man decided to tear them down and build new, bigger barns. "Then," he told himself, "I will sit back and enjoy life for years to come." The man didn't know it, but his dreams of comfort and security would never come true. The same night he mapped out his plan for a life of luxury, his heart gave out and he died. Jesus called the man a fool because he stored up all his treasure for himself and did not have a "rich relationship with God" (Luke 12:21 NLT).

Not once did Jesus imply the man had no relationship with God whatsoever. Nor does He imply the man went straight to hell because of his obsession with the size of his crops. Instead, the man was a fool because he did not have a *rich* relationship with God. He'd wasted his time on earth on that which did not matter, and in the process, he neglected intimacy with His God, leaving him the poorer for it. The sum total of his life's pursuits didn't count for anything.

The Choice

The Bible shows that all of us face a choice. It isn't just a choice between God and the devil or heaven and hell. No, this choice is much more subtle. Each day you and I must choose the kind of treasure to which we will devote our lives. Either we will spend our lives filling the attic and garage with a lifetime of collectibles or we will spend our lives laying up treasure in heaven (Luke 12:33–34). We cannot do both. We can't chase material goods and serve God at the same time. Jesus said that is impossible: "No one can be a slave of two masters, since either he will hate one and love the other, or be devoted to one and despise the other. You cannot be slaves of God and of money" (Matt. 6:24).

I know a lot of people who have tried to find a way to prove this statement false, myself included, without success. When it comes to God and finding security in this world, we want both/and, not either/or. We want to serve God, but we would also like some guarantees about this world, which brings us right back to where we started this chapter. There are no guarantees in this world because no one knows what the future may hold.

Of course, God knows what tomorrow will bring. The future never surprises Him since He lives outside of time. He writes history. How could He ever be caught off guard by it? And He hasn't kept all this knowledge to Himself. Through both the Bible and time He has revealed the essentials every one of us needs to know about the future. Hebrews 9:27 tells us that "it is appointed for people to die once—and after this, judgment"—a fact confirmed by the death rate for the human race that remains at 100 percent. The absence of U-Hauls at funerals also confirms 1 Timothy 6:7, which says, "For we brought nothing into the world, and we can take nothing out."

And, although we do not know what will happen tomorrow, we do know bad things happen to even the godliest people. God placed the Book of Job in the Bible to remind us of this truth just in case we are ever tempted to think otherwise.

The Promise That Makes It Possible

In the midst of this world of uncertainty, God makes another promise: "I will never leave you or forsake you" (Heb. 13:5). No matter what the future may bring, God will always be there for His children. More to the point, we will always be with Him. When you follow Jesus Christ by faith, your real life is hidden with Christ in God (Col. 3:3). Since Jesus sits at the right hand of the Father in heaven, this means our real lives are there in Him.

Heaven isn't just a promise for Christians to look forward to when they die. Our real lives already dwell there even though our bodies made of flesh and blood are still trapped in the physical world of time and space. Not only do we have the assurance that God is with us each and every day as we make our way through this world, we are with Him in the heavenly realm when we belong to His Son. We may be trapped in time, but our real lives are lived in the eternal.

Once we move from the temporal to the eternal, we don't have to worry about the uncertainty of the future. We still don't know what the future may bring, but it no longer matters. Words like "past" and "future" only apply to the world of time. Once we move into the eternal, there is only the present reality of "now." That doesn't mean that today is the only thing that matters, so it's pointless to plan for the future. Instead, living in the eternal realm where our real lives are hidden with Christ in God means we don't have to worry about the uncertainties of life in the world of time.

In Christ we find true security, and nothing the future may hold can change that fact. As Romans 8:38–39 says, "For I am persuaded that neither death nor life, nor angels nor rulers, nor things present, nor things to come, nor powers, nor height, nor depth, nor any other created thing will have the power to separate us from the love of God that is in Christ Jesus our Lord!"

This simple truth sets us free to pursue a life that matters. Yes, we still need food and clothes and shelter, but living in the eternal keeps them in their proper perspective. More important, it keeps them out of our way as we live a life that touches and changes generations to come. Instead of worrying about tomorrow and hoarding money and possessions, we simply trust God to take care of us in this world of time as we serve Him and store up treasures in heaven.

We aren't to trust God for only the *things* we need in this life. Instead, we are to entrust Him with our very lives and leave the rest to Him. Jesus told us to seek God's kingdom above all else and He would take care of our daily needs. That's the definition of faith. And this trust brings the material possessions surrounding us into their proper focus, setting us free to live a life that matters.

Chapter 6

Into Something Beautiful

We all tend to live "ash heap lives";
we spend most of our time and money for
things that will end up in the city dump.
FRANCIS SCHAEFFER, *NO LITTLE PEOPLE*

▪▪

I tell you, use your worldly resources to benefit
others and make friends. In this way, your generosity
stores up a reward for you in heaven.
LUKE 16:9 (NLT)

*J*esus told a story about a rich man who hired a manager
to handle his affairs, but the manager turned out to be a
crook (Luke 16:1–9). As soon as the rich man discovered
the truth about his newest employee, he told him to get his
accounts in order and prepare to be fired. Now this pre-
sented a quandary for the manager. He knew if he lost this
job, he would never be able to find another. (Apparently,
rich people who hired managers in the ancient Middle East
always checked out prospective employees' references.) The
soon-to-be-dismissed manager was too proud to beg, and

he didn't have the strength for the only unskilled manual labor job available to him at the time—ditchdigging.

Knowing his time was short, he hatched a plan. He contacted everyone who owed his boss money and immediately settled their accounts for half of their original debt. Apparently the manager knew he would never be able to get back in his boss's good graces, which was why the manager threw the "get out of debt now" sale. He settled the accounts with his boss's debtors, so that once he lost his job, these guys would be so grateful for what he had done for them, they would help take care of him.

The rich man finds out what his crook of a manager has done and admires him for being so resourceful. Jesus never says the rich guy changes his mind about firing the manager, which leads us to believe that nothing changed in the manager's employment status. The rich man may have admired his manager's tactics, but he still thought he was a crook. Now here's where the story gets a little hard to understand. We expect Jesus to point out how wrong the dishonest manager was and tell us how to avoid the same kind of sin. But he doesn't. Instead Jesus holds up the manager as an example we should follow. Essentially He tells us to go and do likewise, concluding the story with the words, "I tell you, make friends for yourselves by means of the unrighteous money so that when it fails, they may welcome you into eternal dwellings" (Luke 16:9). Jesus said some surprising things, but this pretty much tops them all.

So what's the point? Does Jesus want us to become dishonest crooks who play fast and loose with our employers' ledgers? Hardly. But Jesus does want us to learn the secret the dishonest manager figured out when his back was against the wall. We already know money and anything it can buy will not last. However, through this story Jesus is telling us we can use the temporary things of this world to achieve eternal results. We are to use our money and possessions for the benefit of others, and by doing so, we will win friends and store up for ourselves real treasure in heaven.

Beauty for Ashes

Nothing blocks our pursuit of a life that matters quite like material possessions. The longing for security in an uncertain world and the residual effects of living in an affluent society seep into our souls and pull us away from what we say is most important to us. Yet money and possessions don't have to be a stumbling block. They can become tools with which we can impact the lives of others and store up treasure for ourselves in heaven in the process.

Few ideas found in the Bible are quite as radical as this: that even though this world is passing away, if we use the resources we find in this world properly, they will yield eternal rewards. It's not just that God takes note of how we spend our money (and He does). According to Jesus, when we use material possessions for the benefit of others, we make an impact on their lives they will never forget. Ever. When this life is over, they will be waiting for us in heaven to welcome us home and to thank us for our generosity. Francis Schaeffer put it this way: "If you are a Christian, you are really going to be in Heaven, and some of the people you now know will be there, and they will speak with you about what you did in this life. Somebody will say to you, 'Thank you so much for the money you gave me when my children were starving. I didn't have a chance to thank you then, but I do now.' 'I remember the night you opened your home to me, when you moved over and shared your table with me.' This is what Jesus was saying, and He implied that you are a fool if you do not keep this in mind."[1]

I am far too foolish with my spending because I rarely keep this truth in mind in the course of daily life. If you are like me, and I can't help but think you are, we spend money so casually that we quickly forget where it goes and what we bought with it. This doesn't mean we walk around wasting money. We're just trying to get by. Then again, maybe we are just throwing our money away. Since we live in a culture of accumulation, it is hard to keep from collecting more and more stuff that will eventually be replaced by more stuff. Before long, we lose all track of where our money went— that's how memorable most of our purchases are.

From time to time we need to step back and see the things we keep accumulating in light of eternity. In my office right now is a watch I never wear that I bought for ten dollars while on vacation one year. A couple of baseballs signed by a major league baseball player I once did a book with are on one corner of my desk, while a mug filled with quarters sits on another. An old flashlight that doesn't work lies next to a clock, while a portable CD player gathers dust next to my flatbed scanner. And behind me are stacks and stacks of books. The watch will eventually stop running and be thrown out. The baseballs will probably stay on my desk long enough that any future grandchildren I might have will say "Who?" when I tell about the player who signed them. The flashlight will end up in the trash sooner rather than later along with everything else cluttering my desk. And the stacks of books will keep growing until the day my three daughters have to sort through them after I've left this world.

Looking on the accumulation of assorted items on my desk, I realize Schaeffer was right when he said we spend our time and money on things that will end up in a landfill. A walk through the rest of the house only reinforces his point. Nothing on my desk or in my house and garage will last. I'm not saying I should then give away every scrap of furniture and everything else I own. However, I do need to always keep in mind that not only will this stuff not last, but it will become a distant memory once it is gone. Yet, according to Jesus, when I step away from a lifestyle of accumulation and make generosity my priority, these temporary items give way to permanent treasure. When I invest in people rather than stuff, the way I use my cash suddenly takes on eternal significance. Acts of generosity and kindness live on longer than any other way I could spend my money.

A Lifestyle of Generosity

The story of the crooked manager isn't the only place Jesus tells us we can exchange temporary possessions for eternal treasure. When it comes to money, this is one of the Bible's primary messages. Jesus told the rich young ruler to sell everything He had and give it to the poor as a prerequisite for becoming His follower (Mark 10:21). After telling His disciples not to worry about what they will eat or what they will wear, Jesus told them, "Do not be afraid, little flock, for your Father has chosen gladly to give you the kingdom. Sell your possessions and give to charity; make yourselves money belts which do not wear out, an unfailing treasure in heaven, where no thief comes near nor moth destroys. For where your treasure is, there your heart will be also" (Luke 12:32–34).

Early Christians took these words to heart. In the Book of Acts we're told they "began selling their property and possessions and were sharing them with all, as anyone might have need" (Acts 2:45). By doing so they were putting into action what God has always wanted from His children. One thousand four hundred years before Jesus, Moses wrote, "If there is a poor person among you, one of your brothers within any of your gates in the land the Lord your God is giving you, you must not be hardhearted or tightfisted toward your poor brother. Instead, you are to open your hand to him and freely loan him enough for whatever need he has. . . . Give to him, and don't have a stingy heart when you give, and because of this the Lord your God will bless you in all your work and in everything you do" (Deut. 15:7–8, 10).

God doesn't ask for occasional acts of generosity. Dropping a couple of bucks in the Salvation Army bucket every Christmas isn't enough. When it comes to money, generosity is to be a way of life for those who claim to be His followers. If you think about it, how could we do otherwise if we take seriously all we say we believe? The heart and soul of Christianity is the conviction that God is the maker, owner, and ruler of everything. The entire physical universe belongs to Him and He can do with it anything He pleases.

This doesn't apply only to the planets circling an unnamed star in the far corners of the universe. To claim God owns everything means He also owns everything we usually claim as our own. The house, the car, the computer, that pile of stuff in the corner of the garage that we plan to haul down to Goodwill someday—all of it belongs to God, not us. If we really believe this, then our grip on anything we think of as our own will be very, very loose. Instead of clinging to our stuff, our attitude should be one of constant prayer, asking God, "What are Your plans for this?"

This isn't just a bunch of religious talk. This is how we are to actually live day in and day out as we escape the bonds of the temporal and begin to live in the eternal realm. It's easy to talk about faith when we face a financial crisis in which we need God to come through in an unmistakable way. Anyone can believe in God *for* something. Even the youngest child can ask God for something they want or need. We *should* take our needs to God; I'm not discounting that. However, asking God to give me something without my also surrendering complete control of everything I already have isn't biblical faith. It is little more than American consumerism cloaked in God-talk.

My focus remains on myself, which keeps me from seeing those around me whose needs God wants to meet through me. I'm to share what I have with those in need not just because it is the compassionate thing to do, but because God wants to reveal Himself through my acts of generosity. My life can then impact others through something as simple as giving my second coat to the man who doesn't have even one.

Free at Last

Years ago I owned a classic red 1966 Mustang convertible with a white top. When I first bought it, the seller had to haul it to my house on a flatbed trailer. The engine started, but the transmission was shot. The back of the car was dented in as were a couple of the fenders. And the hood and front bumper were missing. Over the course of a year, I poured myself into that little car. I scoured junkyards for parts and ordered what I could directly from Ford. My parents even bought me a new bumper as a high school graduation present.

Once the restoration process was complete, my work had just begun. I constantly worried someone would steal it or scratch the paint in a parking lot. And then there were the little problems that kept surfacing. The top leaked when I drove in heavy rain and the door locks didn't work like they should. One day while driving back to college, a tooth broke off a gear and I had to rebuild the transmission. Again. Once while on a date with my future wife, a wire came loose under the dashboard. When I pressed in on the clutch at a stoplight the wire shorted out, sparking a small fire. I put out the fire and saved the car, but I spent the next week rewiring it. The car was a classic, and even when I see a Mustang convertible commercial today, part of me wants to turn back the clock. But if the truth were known, I didn't own that little red car. It owned me.

All of our possessions hold the same power over our lives unless we surrender ownership to God. We live in a consumer society, but the consumer isn't who we think it is. The things we accumulate are consuming us; we aren't consuming them. They run our lives, and if I didn't know better, I would say they know it. If you have any doubt as to whether your stuff is eating up your life, just take an honest look at how much of your time and energy goes into accumulating and maintaining it.

I know a man who dreamed of moving his family out into the country where they could live a simpler life. They bought a couple of horses and some sheep and a goat or two. Now he spends all his free time taking care of animals or driving a riding lawn mower around in circles trying to keep the lawn under control. He doesn't have time to play ball with his kids or go on long walks with his wife, the very things he thought he would be able to do in his country home. Instead the house, yard, and animals control his life. They own him.

We don't even have to own things for them to control us. Constantly wanting more—longing to have a bigger house or a nicer car or a faster computer—pulls our attention off of everything else. Before we know it, we're trapped by things we don't yet have. Our out-of-control desires keep us in their grip.

Surrendering control of everything we own sets us free from the tyranny of possessions. It won't keep the lawn from needing to be mowed, but it will alter our decisions about what and why we buy things. When our focus ceases to be on how much we can accumulate and instead moves to how much we can give away for the kingdom of God, material goods no longer possess us. A generous spirit protects us from worrying about holding on to what we have and from plotting how to get more. Instead we are free to concentrate on what really matters in life. The biggest obstacle we face in our quest for a life that matters will be overcome.

Where to Start

It's very easy to spiritualize ideas like using worldly resources to benefit others and surrendering control of everything I own to Christ. I tell myself I've done just that, although evidence shows that my life goes on the way it was before. I agree with my mind that I need to be generous, and by golly, I will turn loose of everything I own. But until I actually take the next step and put generosity into practice as a regular part of my life, I'm still not where I need to be.

As I said earlier, God never meant for all of this instruction to be little more than religious talk. Jesus' words still ring true: "Sell your possessions and give to the poor. Make money-bags for yourselves that won't grow old, an inexhaustible treasure in heaven, where no thief comes near and no moth destroys" (Luke 12:33).

So where do we start? Are we to sell everything we have and give it *all* to the poor? Is Jesus telling me I cannot own *anything* if I plan to be His disciple? Not at all. God knows living on planet Earth means we need food, clothing, shelter, transportation, and other basic necessities. Nor do Jesus' words mean we should never own anything new. Driving a beat-up old Cavalier doesn't make you more spiritual than driving a new Camry would. The key is maintaining an attitude of absolute trust in God and placing everything at His disposal.

Attitudes don't mean much without action, and therein lies the challenge. Before you move on to the next chapter, spend some time taking inventory of your life. Take a long, honest look at your possessions. Which of them have the strongest hold on your life? What has the greatest control over you and your schedule? What do you own that most gets in the way of the life you want to live?

Jesus once said, "If your right eye causes you to sin, gouge it out and throw it away. For it is better that you lose one of the parts of your body than for your whole body to be thrown into hell" (Matt. 5:29). While I don't believe He wanted us to go around yanking our eyeballs out of their sockets, I think the point He was making is clear: whatever blocks the life you truly want to live—a life lived in the eternal rather than in the temporal, a life that rubs off on others and changes the lives of generations—needs to go. Get rid of

Chapter 7

The Power of Contentment

It is difficulties that show what men are.
EPICTETUS

||||||||||||||||||||||||||||||||||||||||||||||||||||||||||||||||||||||||

Give me neither poverty nor riches! Give me just
enough to satisfy my needs. For if I grow rich, I may deny
you and say, "Who is the Lord?" And if I am too poor, I
may steal and thus insult God's holy name.
PROVERBS 30:8–9 (NLT)

Just enough. When God meets a need, He usually provides just enough. No more. No less. At times He pours on the blessings and gives far beyond the need of the moment, but more often than not He gives just enough. He's always operated this way, and He always will.

Nearly thirty-five hundred years ago, the children of Israel marched out of slavery in Egypt and headed toward a land God said flowed with milk and honey. Their new home would be everything they ever dreamed about during their four hundred years of captivity: wide open spaces with green fields for their flocks and herds, olive groves covering the hillsides, and vineyards with grape clusters so large they touched the ground. God promised to give this land to Abraham, Isaac, and Jacob, and after a few hundred years of waiting, the promise was about to come true. However, between the vineyards of the Promised Land and the hardships of Egypt lay hundreds of miles of desert the three or four million Israelites would have to cross on foot. Most of the people making the trip expected to have something to eat along the way, which was no small task in a place where the annual rainfall is measured in millimeters, not inches. The people carried what food they could out of Egypt, but it eventually ran out. That's when God stepped in.

One morning the Israelites went outside and discovered a white substance no one had ever seen before covering the ground. The Israelites called it *manna,* which means "What is it?" God called it the bread from heaven. Through Moses, He told everyone to go out six mornings a week and gather as much as they needed for that day. However, no one was to keep any overnight, except one day a week. God provided a double amount on Fridays, so the people could rest on the Sabbath day. Each day they had to gather what they needed for that day, and they had to do so quickly before the sun rose in the sky and the manna melted into the sand.

A few people ignored God and stuffed some into their tents for later. The next morning the leftover manna was crawling with worms. Finding maggots in their manna was enough for most people to get the point. Every day the people of Israel started their morning the same way. They went outside and gathered manna for the day. "When they measured it by quarts, the person who gathered a lot had no surplus, and the person who gathered a little had no shortage. Each gathered as much as he needed to eat" (Exod. 16:18).

Everyone had just enough, because when God meets a need, He usually gives just enough. No more. No less.

I had my own desert experience several years ago when my wife and I moved our family from California to Indiana with a brief layover in Kentucky. We couldn't afford to hire a moving company since we didn't have jobs awaiting us in Indiana. This move was purely an act of faith—the first and perhaps only time in my life when God placed me in a position where if He didn't come through, there was no Plan B to fall back on. We loaded everything we owned into a moving truck and headed east. My wife drove our minivan with our three daughters inside. The family dog and I rode in the truck. As we passed through Barstow, California, on our first day on the road, my wife radioed me about filling up our gas tanks. If we didn't fill up in Barstow, we wouldn't see another gas station for nearly 150 miles. Between Barstow and the next town, Needles, was nothing but the Mojave Desert. Since the gauge in the truck showed I had nearly three-fourths of a tank of gas, I told my wife to keep going. We were making great time. I didn't see any need to slow down.

Less than twenty minutes later, the needle on the gas gauge started dropping. Quickly. The deeper we drove into the Mojave, the faster the needle plunged. When we went up a hill it dropped down almost to empty. The dog and I prayed our way through the desert. At least I did. The dog would have if she'd known how close we came to becoming a modern-day chapter in *Death Valley Days*. Finally, I coasted into a gas station in Needles. I put fifty-seven gallons in the truck's sixty-gallon gas tank. We could have gone another ten or fifteen miles at the most. But we didn't run out of gas. God gave us just enough.

We shouldn't have been surprised. Over the next several months we experienced the same thing time and time again. We never had a surplus, and many times we didn't know how we would pay the rent until the day it was due, but we always had what we needed. Never more. Never less. Always just enough.

Just Enough Is Not Enough for Most of Us

God never missed a day when He gave the Israelites manna in the desert. His original plan called for them to spend just enough time in the desert for them to learn to depend on Him alone. They failed to learn the lesson and the original two-year plan turned into forty. And every day for forty years God sent manna down from heaven. Each and every morning except the Sabbath, the Israelites gathered up the white, flaky substance that tasted like honey cakes. And each and every day for forty years, they ate the same stuff morning, noon, and night. As you can probably guess, they eventually got so sick of manna that the sight of it made them want to hurl. But God kept right on giving it to them. If He hadn't, they would have starved, and He wouldn't let that happen. He kept providing just enough until the day He took them across the Jordan River and settled them in the land He had promised their forefathers so long before.

I don't think it was just the taste of the manna that got to the Israelites. After all, I know a guy who ate peanut butter sandwiches for lunch every day for more than thirty years at an assembly line job where he did the same task every day. He might have matched the Israelites' forty years of manna if not for the frequent auto industry layoffs during the 1970s.

If this guy could stomach peanut butter for three decades, I figure the Israelites eventually adjusted to an all-manna-all-the-time diet. No doubt they wanted a little variety, and from time to time they would go griping to Moses about their food, but I think they wanted something else as well—something much harder to find in the middle of a desert. They wanted a more secure future than can be found waiting on bread to fall from heaven with the morning dew.

Living hand to mouth, even with God's hand to your mouth, can grow wearisome after awhile. It shouldn't, and maybe it doesn't for the real giants of the faith, but for ordinary strugglers, it does. I know from experience. For the months that followed our family's adventure in the desert, we had to depend on God's impeccable timing for everything. My wife and I both worked, but decent jobs were hard to come by for a full-time graduate student and a stay-at-home mom. I mowed yards and my wife cleaned houses, but at the end of the day, we both knew we didn't make nearly enough to cover our basic expenses. But God gave us just what we needed when we needed it. Whether we had to pay for car insurance or for cereal, when the deadline arrived, so did God's provision.

Through this time, our faith grew like it never had before. We learned more about God and His faithfulness in those months than we had before or have since. And yet, we couldn't wait for those days to end. We all cheered when a church called and offered me a job paying more than I'd made in the California church we'd left. I knew God would provide just what I needed, but I was anxious to have a little cushion at the end of each month. I wanted more than just enough.

I'm not alone. Jesus told us not to worry about what we will wear or eat. He said His Father already knows what we need and will take care of us. But most of us don't want the minimum provision. Give us today our daily bread, Jesus taught His disciples to pray, but how many of us are satisfied with living on bread alone? Not many.

It's not just the desire for security that drives us. We live in a culture incapable of denying itself anything. Everywhere we turn we hear the same message: we need more and lots of it. And most of us have bought into the message. On average, Americans spend $1.22 for every dollar they earn.[1] God may provide just enough, but we've perfected living beyond our means into an art form. According to the Federal Reserve, consumer debt reached $2.1 trillion in December 2004.[2] That figure does not include mortgages or home-equity loans. All told, the average U.S. household with a mortgage, two college graduates who borrowed money for school, and more than one credit card, now owes about $112,000—a number that is expected to rise.[3]

Enough Is Enough

When it comes to debt, you are probably average or above. That's why you picked up a book on simplifying and downsizing your life. Most of the stress that makes us feel the need to change our lifestyles comes either through our finances or our schedules. We're worn out from trying to make ends meet with a mortgage, college loans, car loans, and credit card bills, along with the frenzy of trying to squeeze everything we want to do into the space of each twenty-four-hour period. *So show me how to get my life under control,* you say. *Take me to that simpler life where I don't have to worry about money 24/7.*

You've already read about how you need to lean on God for your security rather than on your possessions. The last chapter told you to give stuff away, so that your possessions will stop possessing you. The final key to simplifying your financial life and keeping material goods from blocking a life that matters is just as simple: be content with what you have. Let God's just enough be enough.

The endless cycle of wanting more keeps us from ever being able to sit back and enjoy this life. Solomon said, "Those who love money will never have enough. How absurd to think that wealth brings true happiness!" (Eccles. 5:10 NLT). But as Paul wrote, "Godliness with contentment is a great gain" (1 Tim. 6:6). When we choose to be content, we are able to accept and rejoice in whatever situation we find ourselves. Instead of worrying about every possibility lurking around the corner, we leave the future in God's hand and trust He knows what He is doing.

Contentment means choosing to believe God when He says He knows what we need before we know it ourselves and accepting whatever He provides as good enough. In Philippians 4:6–7, contentment means: "Don't worry about anything, but in everything, through prayer and petition with thanksgiving, let your requests be made known to God. And the peace of God, which surpasses every thought, will guard your hearts and your minds in Christ Jesus."

The key to enjoying life is choosing to be content with whatever God provides rather than craving more.

Is God Holding Out on Us?

There's only one problem with this whole contentment thing. By saying I must choose to let God's just enough be enough, it almost sounds like God is holding out on us. The Bible says God owns the cattle on a thousand hills

(Ps. 50:10), which is an ancient way of saying God's riches cannot be measured. Doesn't He want to share the wealth with us? After all, in the Old Testament He didn't force the Israelites to eat manna forever. Once they arrived in the Promised Land, God gave them flocks and herds and everything else their hearts desired. They moved into houses they didn't build and enjoyed the fruit of groves and vineyards they didn't plant.

If God is the same yesterday, today, and forever (Heb. 13:8), isn't it safe to assume He will do the same for us today? After all, aren't we God's children? What good parents don't give their kids the best they have? Jesus Himself said, "If you then, who are evil, know how to give good gifts to your children, how much more will your Father in heaven give good things to those who ask Him!" (Matt. 7:11). Why should we settle for just enough when it sounds like God wants to give us so much more?

We shouldn't. That's why God's blessings cannot be measured in terms of this world. God not only wants to give us more, He's already given it to us. The first chapter of Paul's letter to the church in Ephesus tells us God has blessed us with every spiritual blessing heaven can hold. Galatians tells us that as God's children, His entire estate belongs to us. Romans calls us heirs with Christ who will one day share in God's glory. First Peter assures us God has reserved a priceless inheritance for us in heaven that will never rust or fade away. And the last book of the Bible, Revelation, describes a city with streets of gold that will one day be ours.

All of this is not just a bunch of religious mumbo jumbo. Whether we want to admit it or not, this is *the* truth upon which we must build our lives. This world (which seems so permanent) is temporary, but the world we cannot see, the eternal realm where God dwells, is the real world. When you belong to Jesus Christ, the eternal is your real home. There you are rich beyond your wildest imagination. Unlike the temporary riches of this world, the wealth we possess in eternity is real wealth. It will not fade with time, nor will a downturn in the stock market take any of it away. This wealth will last forever.

Therefore, choosing to be satisfied with whatever God provides in this temporary world of time doesn't mean we're settling for less than what we could have. Instead, this choice recognizes the fact that we have true wealth waiting for us at home. We can put up with less than ideal situations, because we know we don't belong here and we aren't going to stay here. We're just passing through this world of time.

When I was nine years old, my family drove from Oklahoma to northern California to see my mother's brother and his family. On the trip home, we drove into Salt Lake City, where we planned to spend the night. We ran into one small problem: every hotel room in the city was booked due to a convention in town. We kept driving, looking for a place to stay, but towns are few and far between in northern Utah. Finally, at about 2:00 a.m., my dad found an old hotel in a town in Wyoming where the sidewalks were still made of wood.

This hotel lacked the usual amenities other hotels offer. If memory serves, it was a dump. The room was old and dingy. My mother and sisters slept on top of the covers since they were afraid of what they might find lurking between the sheets. The bathroom was down the hall, and the air-conditioning consisted of a brick propping the window open. But after driving half the night, none of us cared. Besides, it wasn't like we planned to live in the room for the rest of our lives. We were just passing through.

That's how we need to see this world. When we belong to Jesus Christ, we don't belong to this world of time. Peter calls us strangers and aliens. We're out of place here. Heaven is our real home. This conviction allows us to be content with whatever situation we may find ourselves in now. In the long run, whatever we face here on earth doesn't really matter, because it isn't like we plan on sticking around this place forever. Just a moment or two in heaven and we will forget about any supposed hardships we faced here.

Best of Both Worlds

Knowing all of this, I still have to ask why God gives us just enough rather than more than we could ask for. I know I will go to heaven someday because of the grace God poured out on me through Jesus Christ. This world is not my home; I'm just passing through. I get that. But why does the trip here have to be so Spartan? If this life were a rental car, wouldn't it be just as easy for God to make it a new Cadillac Escalade as a 1972 Ford Pinto?

The answer is, of course, He could. And occasionally He does. However, because God loves us, He gives us what we really need, and the one thing we need more than anything else is to depend on Him at every moment of every day. He wants us to know Him and enjoy Him forever. Unfortunately, most human beings have a tendency to marginalize God when times are good. The more we have, the less we think we need God and the more we believe this world is our home.

I'll admit it: I want the best of both worlds. If given the choice between the best of heaven and the best of earth, I would choose both. But time and again my life shows I can't handle both. My prayer life grows anemic when life sails along smoothly. But let the slightest blip come my way—let a pile of unexpected bills land in my mailbox or a sudden pain strike one of my children—and I'm on my knees.

I'm not alone. After Israel moved into the Promised Land and started enjoying God's very best, they soon forgot all about Him. They may not have liked depending on God to give them manna every morning, but they stayed closer to Him when they had to rely on Him for their basic needs every moment of every day.

In Proverbs 30:8–9 a wise man named Agur son of Jakeh prayed, "Give me neither poverty nor wealth; feed me with the food I need. Otherwise, I might have too much and deny You, saying, 'Who is the Lord?' or I might have nothing and steal, profaning the name of my God."

This should be our prayer as well. *O God, give me just enough to provide what I need in this world, but not so much that I would ever mistake this world for my true home. Lord, I need food to eat and clothes to wear and a roof over my head, but please give me just enough to always remember my greatest need is You.* This is the prayer of contentment. It is the key to finding the life we've always wanted.

Chapter 8

But I Live in the Real World

You have nothing to show for all the money you've earned over the past twenty years except a heavily mortgaged house; a car that you owe twenty-seven more payments on, even though it's already showing symptoms of Fatal Transmission Disease; numerous malfunctioning appliances; huge mounds of books you never read; records you never listen to; clothes you never wear; and membership cards to health clubs you never go to; and—somewhere in the depths of your refrigerator—a year-old carton half-filled with a substance that may once have been mu-shu pork.

DAVE BARRY, *DAVE BARRY TURNS 40*

▪▪

*To enjoy your work and accept your lot in life—
that is indeed a gift from God. People who do
this rarely look with sorrow on the past,
for God has given them reasons for joy.*

ECCLESIASTES 5:19–20 (NLT)

*B*ooks like this one often do a great disservice to readers. We authors tell you to radically alter your lifestyle.

Stop depending on material possessions for your security! we shout. *Trust in God instead.* Then we tell you to stop hoarding and instead adopt a lifestyle of generosity. *And be content,* we add. *Accept God's just enough as enough, for contentment is the key to really enjoying life.* Above all, we tell you to move your focus off of the world of time and place it squarely on eternity.

However, if I stop here, I haven't done you any favors. Something is still missing from the equation. Talking about focusing on the eternal is great and wonderful and all of that, but, you and I still live in the world of time. We need to know what all of this will look like in the real world. How do our lives need to change to put this into practice?

If I don't answer that question, this book will most likely lead to greater frustration and guilt rather than genuine freedom. Yet, by exploring the answer I also risk steering you onto a path that isn't any better than the lifestyle of consumption most of us are already trapped in. When discussions of simplifying our lifestyles, especially our financial lifestyles, turn to practical lists of "do this" and "don't do that," we risk turning this entire enterprise into mechanical legalism. You can do everything I mention here—and the list is far from all-inclusive—and still miss the point of this book.

The Bible says everything that does not come from faith is sin (Rom. 14:23). That means you can live a good life and be the nicest guy the world has ever known, but if you don't live by faith in the God of the universe, your good deeds don't mean a thing. The same is especially true here. You can get your financial house in order, but if everything you do doesn't begin with a faith relationship with God and a lifestyle of trusting in Him at every moment of every day, your efforts are for naught.

The goal of bringing order to the life you live in the material world goes back to what we really want out of life. Your life and mine can be used by God to touch and change generations. Our lives can matter when they are spent on that which lasts. That is why we need to bring order to our checkbooks and the growing pile of stuff filling our pantries, closets, attics, and garages. We still have to live in this world of time, which means we will still have to pay water bills and electric bills and all those other bills we would rather live without. But by making some basic changes in our daily lives, we can keep the demands of the physical world from blocking what we really want to do in this life.

With this in mind, we now proceed cautiously. Again, none of what follows are meant to be taken as rules carved in stone. Nor should these insights be seen as a standard of spirituality, as though by clearing out closets for the poor, you are somehow more spiritual than the person who doesn't.

These are suggestions for getting your life in order. Hopefully, many will seem difficult. At least they seemed difficult to me as I wrote them. I'm struggling right beside you to put them in place in my daily life. These suggestions should seem hard, for they all flow out of Jesus' command to deny ourselves. Saying no to ourselves is never fun. As Francis Schaeffer said, "We are surrounded by a culture that says 'no' to nothing. When we are surrounded with this sort of mentality, in which everything is to be judged by bigness and success, then suddenly to be told that in the Christian life there is to be this strong negative aspect of saying 'no' to things and 'no' to self, it must seem hard. And if it does not feel hard to us, we are not really letting it speak to us."[1]

With that in mind, I now offer the following ten suggestions for making simplicity a vital part of your daily life.

1. Live below your means, rather than beyond them

Years ago while sitting in small-group Bible study, one couple asked the rest of us to pray with them about a decision with which they were wrestling. They'd just had their first child, and the wife desperately wanted to stay home with the baby. But she had a good job and, they told us, it took both of their incomes to make ends meet. Everyone in the room nodded as they shared their request. We all knew what they were going through. We were all young and no one had been married for more than a few years. Those of us who didn't yet have children knew we would face the exact same choice. It was just a matter of time.

But all of our smiles and empathetic nods were disrupted by a voice from the small-group leader. "So lower your standard of living," he said. "Then you will be able to get by on one income." An audible gasp filled the room. These words were so blunt, they caught all of us by surprise. Yet I've never forgotten them, because he was right. If this young middle-class couple from a nice suburb in Dallas, Texas, were really serious about not taking their child to the baby-sitter every morning, they would do whatever it took to make their desire a reality, even if that meant doing without many of the things to which they'd grown accustomed.

Isn't that true for all of us? I don't know anyone who doesn't want to de-stress their financial lives. Most of us feel stretched to the absolute limit. The checkbook and bill drawer fills our hearts with dread and our lives with fear. But at the same time, we don't want to do without many of the things in life we take for granted. The bottom line is this: we cannot have it all. Bringing order to our financial house means doing without some things we want to gain that which we absolutely need. And that demands living below our means rather than beyond them.

I know, this is easier said than done. However, most of us waste a great deal of money every month without realizing it. Look through the checks you write each month and ask yourself, *How much do I really need this?* I know ESPN or HGTV feel like necessities, but is the monthly cable bill really worth the stress it places on your monthly budget? The same goes for the grocery store. Something as simple as using a list and placing a strict limit on what you will spend each week can save you hundreds of dollars a year. My oldest daughter taught me to shop for groceries with a list in one hand and a calculator in the other. Once she reaches her weekly limit, she either stops shopping or she takes things out of her cart that she could live without. Following her example has allowed my wife and I to reduce our weekly grocery bill by $35. That may not seem like a lot to you, but it comes out to $150 per month, or about $1,800 a year. When things get tight, that money comes in handy.

Living below our means forces us to reevaluate every purchase from light bulbs to cell phones to cars to houses. Rather than stretching your budget to the limit, pull back. Spend less than you make. Remember, the average American spends $1.22 for every dollar earned. For most of us, simply living within our means will demand cuts in our lifestyles. Again, it all comes down to a simple question: What do you really want out of life anyway? When a lifestyle of consumption robs us of fulfilling our purpose for living, cutting back on things like eating out or buying clothes is an easy choice to make.

2. Buy things for their usefulness rather than their status

When Bill Clinton first came to office, he was criticized for wearing a Timex Ironman Decathlon watch rather than a Rolex or some other more "presidential" watch. Clinton's Timex now sits in the Smithsonian Museum. Most people don't care what kind of watch our president wears, just as long as he gets where he needs to be on time. That should be our attitude about all of our possessions. People may judge us by the clothes we wear, the cars we drive, even the watches we wear, but at the end of the day, who cares what they think?

We all have to buy some necessities for life in this world. When you do, buy things for their usefulness rather than the status they may convey. Look for value, not trends. I'm in my midforties, which makes this easy for me to say, but it is still true. Buying a car because it will impress the neighbors is absurd. Choose a car that will give you the most for your money. That doesn't always mean you should buy the cheapest thing available. Cheap doesn't always translate into value. Get the most out of your money and buy what is useful, not what will impress people you don't know or like.

3. Don't believe the hype

"You want everything, don't you?" an ad in my favorite magazine reads. That pretty well sums up the approach of all advertisements in America. Ads tell us what we want, and they have a way of turning that want into a need. That's why an army of eight-year-old boys like me talked our mothers into buying us P. F. Flyers during the 1960s. I, for one, absolutely had to have some P. F. Flyers, because I needed to be able to run faster and jump higher. Every eight-year-old boy believed that's what a pair of P. F. Flyers on our feet would help us do, because the ads that ran during reruns of *Leave It to Beaver* told us just that.

The only way to fully escape the consumer culture surrounding us is to tune out or turn off the barrage of ads coming our way. Take all of their claims with a block of salt. Look through the clever marketing routines and examine the real message. Most ads try to convince us our lives will be somehow happier if we buy their product. Don't believe it. I know a family that yells, "Yeah, right!" back at the television every time an ad makes an outlandish claim. I don't know if talking back to the television is the best way to deprogram ourselves from the constant sales pitches coming our way, but it can't hurt.

4. De-accumulate

We live in a culture of accumulation. Therefore, the best way to escape its grip is to do just the opposite. Rather than buying more and more, begin de-accumulating. Give things away. Cleaning out the mountain of clothes and other things you no longer use is a good place to start, but don't stop there. Discover the joy of giving gifts from things that you still use. One of the greatest gifts I ever received was a set of books that was no longer available in hardcover. A close friend gave me his set as a going-away present when my family moved to California. When he handed them to me, I asked, "Won't you still read these? How can you give them away?" His response still rings in my ears more than fifteen years later: "I would rather give them to you." That's the spirit of de-accumulation.

De-accumulating also means not buying things unless

and until you actually need them. Compulsive purchases rarely translate into a wise use of resources. When you buy things, use them until they need to be replaced. Most of us use things until we get tired of them, even though they are still very useful. That's how a woman I know ended up with ten bottles of shampoo under her sink. Use what you buy and once it has outlasted its usefulness, get rid of it. Sure, that fried-chicken bucket with the picture of a NASCAR driver on the side might be worth something someday, but do you really want to keep it around for decades to find out?

5. Spend wisely. See your money as God's possession, not yours

During Thanksgiving last year, I learned a check I thought would arrive at that time would not be mailed until late January or early February. Since I am self-employed, that was like walking into my boss's office and learning I wouldn't get paid again for the rest of the year (and that all Christmas bonuses had been canceled). Needless to say, this wasn't exactly good news.

Since I was preparing to write this book at the time, I had to actually put into practice everything you've been reading—things like trusting God and letting His enough be enough. I suspected God might be trying to teach me something in the same way that I suspected that the Colts' playoff loss to the Patriots would keep them out of the Super Bowl.

I was still trying to come to grips with all of this one Sunday morning when one of my daughters (who loves cereal) informed me that we were out of milk. I had all of three dollars in cash, which I needed to stretch as far as I could, but I also knew the breakfast of champions required milk. The day before, my wife spoke at a women's retreat and shared how during a similar period in our lives years earlier, God miraculously provided a box of Cocoa Pebbles for my three girls when we could barely afford groceries.

So with all this swirling around in my mind, I trudged down to the local convenience store with the cheapest milk prices to buy a gallon of milk with my last three dollars. When I walked up to the counter, I pulled out my "milk card" for the clerk to punch. The card gives you a free gallon of milk after you buy ten. With this gallon I would be up to four punches. But the clerk informed me that they no longer used the milk cards. Instead, the station had a new rewards program, and because I didn't yet know about the change, she punched the rest of the slots on my milk card, gave me back my three dollars, and handed me a free gallon of milk. It was God's way of telling me He was aware of even my smallest needs.

This episode had a strange side effect. At least it seemed strange to me. The three one-dollar bills took on a whole new significance. For years I've talked about how God owns everything we possess, but for perhaps the first time in my life, I attached this truth to three bills in my wallet. I couldn't spend them on just anything. This was God's money. Since He gave it back to me, I felt He must have some purpose for it. Keep in mind that I am a father of three teenagers. Cash doesn't last long in my wallet, especially during the school year. But one week after the milk episode, those three one-dollar bills still sat in my wallet. God again told me He would make what He gave us last during this dry time as we waited for my check to arrive.

This long story has a point: we should spend our money wisely, treating it like it belongs to God, since it does. I can blow money with the best of them, but when I look into my wallet and see God's money sitting there, everything changes. I may be able to waste my money, but I don't want to waste His.

6. Leave room for extravagance

I know a man who spent more than three hundred dollars on a miniature dachshund puppy for his wife's fortieth birthday. Having grown up in a family that always had mutts that never cost us a dime, I thought this was a little nuts. I asked him, "How can you possibly justify spending that much money on a dog?"

He replied, "I didn't spend that much money on a dog. I spent it on a gift my wife has always wanted."

Needless to say, he bought her the perfect gift. Did he waste his money? I don't think so. Using our resources wisely does not mean we never splurge. God sometimes splurges on us and there are times we should splurge on others.

7. Invest your resources in people, not stuff

People mean more than plasma televisions or new cars. If this is true, then we should invest our money in them. Jesus said, "Where your treasure is, there your heart will be also" (Matt. 6:21). The best way to have a heart for people, then, is to invest our treasures in them.

For families, this means spending money on things that will draw you closer and build the bonds of love between you. I believe there is no better way to do this than by going on vacation together. Take trips that will enable you to build memories and help you get to know one another better. The trips do not have to be extravagant, but they should be memorable. I've found it is better to do without some extras throughout the year to save money for a family trip in the summer.

Another way to invest in people is to set aside money that can be used to answer someone else's prayer. Save and listen closely to the people God places in your life. When you hear them share genuine needs or an opportunity God has given them, use what you've saved to invest in them. Send someone on a mission trip they've longed to take but cannot afford or secretly give them the money they need to get a new business off the ground. Let your imagination run wild and look for creative ways to allow God to work through you to meet the needs of others. As you do, check your ego at the door. Don't invest for thanks or praise. If you find you crave those things, give anonymously so all the credit goes to God. Put your money where your heart is, and when your heart longs to make an eternal difference in the lives of others, what better investment could you possibly find?

8. Give to your local church

God owns everything. He doesn't need our money. However, we need to give to Him as an exercise of faith and an expression of our dependence on Him. In the Old Testament, the people of Israel were to bring one-tenth of their income to the Lord. This was a called a tithe. The New Testament doesn't use a percentage to tell us how much we should give. Instead we find we are to give generously and cheerfully (2 Cor. 9:6–7).

9. Enjoy what you have as a gift from God

"Every generous act and every perfect gift is from above, coming down from the Father of lights," James 1:17

tells us. And that is how we are to view everything we have. Whatever you have, enjoy it as a gift from God. Often when we focus on using money wisely, we forget to enjoy what we have. Solomon wrote in Ecclesiastes 3:13, "And people should eat and drink and enjoy the fruits of their labor, for these are gifts from God" (NLT). Looking at everything you have as a gift from God leads you to a life of constantly giving thanks rather than longing for more. Paul had this in mind when he wrote, "Rejoice always! Pray constantly. Give thanks in everything, for this is God's will for you in Christ Jesus" (1 Thess. 5:16–18).

10. Avoid becoming a legalistic jerk

Remember that the way you use the material resources God places in your hands should reflect faith, generosity, and contentment. When we begin to see our lives as superior or more spiritual than others because of the way we use our money, we haven't simplified our lives; we've just made ourselves unbearable to be around. Richard Foster wrote, "Of all the Disciplines simplicity is the most visible and therefore the most open to corruption."[2] Always keep that in mind and be on your guard. Life consists of more than our possessions, and our spiritual life must consist of more than the way we use them.

This list is far from exhaustive, but I've found these ten suggestions keep me very busy in my effort to clear every obstacle out of a life that matters. Nothing trips us up like our material possessions. However, bringing these under control brings us closer to the life that matters. The next step may be even more difficult because it requires even more discipline, even more saying no to ourselves and those around

Slower

Chapter 9

Courtney Dreads Christmas

*The only reason for time is so that
everything doesn't happen at once.*
ALBERT EINSTEIN

|||||||||||||||||||||||||||||||||||||||||||||||||||||||

*Be very careful, then, how you live—
not as unwise but as wise, making the most of
every opportunity, because the days are evil.*
EPHESIANS 5:15–16 (NIV)

Courtney dreads Christmas. If it were up to her, December 25 would be struck from the calendar. It's not that she has anything against celebrating Jesus' birth. But the day is anything but a time of celebration, unless you enjoy celebrating on the road. She and her husband, Jim, spend most of their holidays crammed into a car with their two sons and boxes of gifts, sprinting back and forth between relatives' homes. Peace on earth it's not, and by the end of the day, she is fresh out of goodwill toward men.

The funny thing is, neither Courtney nor Jim ever planned this. They never sat down one November day and said to one another, "Let's figure out a way to make our holidays as crazy and stressful as humanly possible." No one ever plans to be run ragged in the name of spreading holiday cheer. Somehow it just happens. And Courtney and Jim feel absolutely powerless to do anything about it.

Two years ago Jim almost worked up the nerve to phone his grandmother and say they would not be at her house by eight in the morning for the traditional family Christmas breakfast. He went so far as to dial the number, but he hung up before anyone could answer. "We're family . . ." he shrugs without finishing his sentence. He doesn't have to. Holidays are family time, and if he and Courtney plan on getting along with their families during the other eleven months of the year, they better carve out a large swath of time for them during Christmas.

And they do. From midafternoon Christmas Eve to nine o'clock Christmas night, they visit at least seven different houses for seven different Christmases. Somewhere in between, early on Christmas morning, their sons manage to unwrap the gifts under their own Christmas tree. But they don't have time to actually play with any of their new toys, at least not for a day or two. By then Courtney and Jim are back at work and the baby-sitter does most of the assembly required and exchanges D-cell batteries for C-cells.

That's why Courtney hates Christmas. She isn't Scrooge's great niece but one harried mother, wishing she could find a way to actually enjoy the holidays while building memories with her children. Maybe someday she will. Maybe someday she will work up the nerve to tell her mother they will not be at her house for Christmas brunch. Maybe someday she'll tell her father and stepmother to make plans without them because she and Jim and the boys plan on doing nothing but turning their living room into the biggest Legoland this side of Toys "R" Us.

Maybe someday she'll tell her grandmother that she is cooking her own Christmas dinner in her own kitchen for her own family of four. But not this year. And probably not next. Or the next. Courtney feels trapped by holidays so jam-packed with activity that she can never do what she wants or concentrate on what matters most to her. Enjoying the holidays is her dream. Enduring them comes closer to reality.

Joel loves being a father. He relished the day his two children were born, and he and his wife, Tammy, hung onto every moment they could as their children progressed from diapers to sippy cups to starting school. Sometimes Joel wonders how the years could go by so fast, which only motivates him to reserve even more family time now that his children are in high school. "We know we don't have that much time left before they go off to college and then go out on their own," he says, "so we try to do as many things as we can together now."

But Joel and Tammy face a rival for their children's time they never expected: the local high school. The school day may run from 8:15 a.m. to 3:10 p.m., but that's only the beginning for their two children. The youngest, Mark, plays football, which has now become a twelve-month-per-year commitment. Weight training goes until 5:30 every afternoon, and the week before Valentine's Day, the team started speed training every morning at 6:30. Cassie plays basketball, which also has a demanding schedule. She is also a class officer and serves as the treasurer for the student council. Those responsibilities require her to go to school early two days a week and pull her away from the family several week-ends a year for mandatory events.

She was almost kicked off student council because she went to church with the family one Sunday instead of going with the student council to a fund-raiser they had planned. Joel couldn't believe they scheduled something on a Sunday, but most youth activities now run seven days a week. It was even worse when Mark played on a traveling baseball team when he was twelve. They would play eight or nine games in one weekend, sometimes in towns two and three hours away.

The problem, as Joel sees it, is a lack of perspective in every coach or student activity sponsor. "The football coach constantly preaches commitment to the boys, which is all well and good, but he comes across as though the foot-ball team is the single most important thing in the entire world. He demands two hours both before and after school throughout the off-season, and if a kid doesn't give it, he won't make the team." Joel pauses. "Off-season," he laughs. "When it comes to kids' sports, there aren't any off-seasons any more."

Now Joel and Tammy are left scrambling to find family time in between the hectic schedules of their fourteen- and sixteen-year-olds. They also want to get their kids involved in their church's youth group. Of course, that means another night of everyone in the family going in different directions. Joel isn't sure what to do. "My kids spend eleven hours a day at the school, five days a week, plus at least half a day on Sat-urdays. Tammy and I feel like we spend all of our time just trying to undo a lot of what happens up there, but we're los-ing ground." Joel sighs. "And then I think of how little time we have left before college, and it makes me wonder what the solution can possibly be. I don't know what to do."

Ted was thankful for the job when he found it. The pay was good and he didn't have to relocate his family to stay in his field of expertise—two perks that aren't easy to come by in a state that has been hit particularly hard by outsourcing. He knew he would have to travel occasionally, and early on he worked more nights than he really wanted, but he thought he had to do it to establish himself within the company. A year and a half after signing on, he is still thankful for the job. Many people he knows have been out of work for a long time. Some friends from his church have had to move to keep their jobs with a major manufacturer after it sold a local factory, and the high-paying union jobs were replaced with nonunion positions at roughly half the hourly rate of pay. All in all, Ted feels lucky to have a good job in his hometown, especially when he looks around at the economic hardships so many others are going through.

But that doesn't stop him from growing more and more frustrated by how little time his job leaves for him to have a life. Ted still has to work more nights than he wants, and the travel has become more frequent than he was first led to believe. The work itself is OK. Ted feels confident in what he does, but his boss keeps putting more and more pressure on Ted and the other guys in his division. These aren't the 1990s, when business boomed and money flowed. Every sale comes harder, and reaching production levels of just a few years ago takes more and more time.

Lately Ted has started wondering if the price the job demands is really worth it. "I never feel like I have enough time for my wife and son," he says. "The whole time I'm on the road, I can't help but think how I should be home. But I don't have a lot of choice, not if I want to keep a roof over our heads and food on the table."

Even with his busy work schedule, Ted stays involved in his local church. He leads one of the ministry teams, which means he has to arrive early before the first service on Sunday mornings and stay through the third service. Twice a month he also attends board meetings, and the first Saturday of the month he goes to a men's breakfast. Ted never complains. If anything, he wishes he could find more time for his church, but he doesn't know how that would be possible.

Time is Ted's most precious commodity. He never has enough for what he really wants to do, but he feels there's nothing he can do about it. After all, good jobs are hard to come by, especially in unstable economic times. So Ted keeps traveling. He keeps working more nights than he wishes he had to. And he keeps wondering if there is a way off of this merry-go-round he's trapped on.

On Your Mark . . . Get Set . . . Go!

Every little kid dreams of the day his parents and teachers won't be able to boss him around. *When I'm grown up,* he tells himself, *I will do whatever I want.* But then he grows up and finds out what the rest of us have already learned: no one gets to do whatever they want. At least not most of the time.

Mrs. Marshall, the evil third grade teacher who liked to drag eight-year-old boys to the principal's office, may not be around to yell at you and tell you to keep your hands to yourself and get to work on that English assignment, but she seems tame compared to the voices that took her place when you became an adult. Time pressure never comes from only one source. We feel it from our families and on the job. There's always too much to do and too little time to get it done. A recent poll found 60 percent of all Americans felt pressured to work too much, and more than 80 percent felt they had too little time to spend with their families.[1]

Instead of doing what we want when we want to do it, we run and run and run. To work. To church. To baseball practices and games and guitar lessons and meetings with teachers at the school. The pace grows more and more frantic with each passing year. In the midst of all the running around, we find ourselves wondering if all of this running is accomplishing anything. It is a good question to ask.

Speed is the enemy of influence. For one life to rub off on another and make an impact that lasts for generations, you need time. Lots of time. This isn't an activity that can be squeezed in at 4:15 on a Tuesday afternoon between soccer practice and ballet lessons. One life influences another through relationships and spending quality time together. But rushing around from one meeting to another, one appointment to another, one practice after another, leaves neither the time nor the energy to build much of anything. You end up becoming little more than intimate strangers with those who happen to ride in the car together while trying to keep up the pace.

Using Time Wisely

Every human being faces the same dilemma: all of us are given only twenty-four hours a day, 365 days a year, and a limited number of years per lifetime into which we must squeeze everything we were born to accomplish. At the time the New Testament was written, the average life expectancy at birth was only twenty-two to twenty-five years.[2] This number is made lower by high infant mortality rates, but even those who survived childhood lived much shorter lives than we do today.

In fact, according to the Centers for Disease Control, life expectancies have never been longer than they are now. A child born in the United States today can expect to live, on average, nine years longer than those born just fifty years ago.[3] We may wonder how we can get everything done in one twenty-four-hour period, yet God has entrusted more twenty-four-hour periods to this generation than any that has come before. Jesus said, "Much will be required of everyone who has been given much. And even more will be expected of the one who has been entrusted with more" (Luke 12:48). Since we will live longer than any generation before us, God will hold us more responsible for how we use the time He's given us. The question we then face is not how we can get everything done in the brief amount of time we have here, but how can we keep from wasting the precious time we have on earth.

Time pressure is not a twenty-first-century phenomenon. Paul addressed it in his letter to the Ephesians: "Pay careful attention, then, to how you walk—not as unwise people but as wise—making the most of the time, because the days are evil" (Eph. 5:15–16). People in the first century faced many of the same schedule pressures we face today.

We tend to look back on the past as a simpler time when people had plenty of hours to build rich relationships. It wasn't that way at all. Most of the people to whom Paul wrote were poor. Many were slaves. On top of this, taxes were high, the demands of Rome could be extreme, and scratching out a living in the dry, arid environment wasn't easy. Just surviving took a great deal of time, much less thinking about squeezing in time to go and make disciples and serve God by serving others. Throw in family pressures on top of everything else, and our lives look easier in comparison.

The solution, according to Paul, is to live wisely. Wisdom solves the dilemma of an out-of-control schedule. Rather than bouncing around from one time demand to the next, wisdom allows us to chart a course toward that which we really want out of life. It will not, however, make us exempt from the craziness of life. Nothing can do that at all times. The uncertainties of life and the constant surprises that pop up at the most inopportune moments will never be eliminated.

Some of us hope to find some perfect state of calm and rest where our lives are never harried or hurried. Forget it. That place doesn't exist—at least not in this world. Living wisely means orienting our lives around that which is most important to us and learning to recognize the opportunities God gives us to reach our goals.

Achieving what we really want out of life will not happen without effort on our part. Any goal worth reaching always requires hard work and sacrifice. The bigger the goal, the more work required. What greater goal can anyone possibly find than influencing lives in a way that changes both the eternal destiny of individuals and the lives of generations to come? This won't just happen as we spin along in the dizzy whirl of life. To reach your goal, you must put wisdom into practice each and every day as you invest the precious commodity called time.

Chapter 10

Time

*Time is the coin of your life. It is the only
coin you have, and only you can determine
how it will be spent. Be careful lest you let
other people spend it for you.*

CARL SANDBURG

▬▬▬▬▬▬▬▬▬▬▬▬▬▬▬▬▬▬▬▬▬

*Teach us to make the most of our time,
so that we may grow in wisdom.*

PSALM 90:12 (NLT)

*E*veryone dies. They always have, and everyone knows
they always will. Everyone, that is, except Ray Kurzweil.
A computer scientist and inventor, Kurzweil believes man-
kind is on the brink of a series of incredible technological
breakthroughs that will make death obsolete. In his book
Fantastic Voyage: Live Long Enough to Live Forever, he
and coauthor Terry Grossman see a day when microscopic
robots known as "nanobots" will swim through our blood-
streams, making needed repairs to all our vital organs, thus
allowing us to live forever. Until then, Kurzweil says it is
possible to prevent nearly 90 percent of the maladies that
kill us, including heart disease, cancer, diabetes, kidney and
liver disease through changes in our diets, along with taking

specific nutritional supplements. He also believes recent discoveries will make it possible for us to reprogram the 20,000 to 30,000 genes in the human body, slowing or perhaps stopping our body from degenerating.

Before you pass him off as a total nutcase, you should know Ray Kurzweil received the 1999 National Medal of Technology Award and was inducted into the Inventors Hall of Fame in 2002. He also received the Lemelson-MIT prize, which bills itself as the Academy Award for inventors. The *Christian Science Monitor* called him a young Edison. His inventions include the first reading machine for the blind that was capable of reading any typeface. Many of his earlier predictions regarding the advancement of intelligent machines have come true, though Kurzweil isn't one to sit around gazing into a crystal ball. Instead he says all his predictions are based on solid methodology and careful observation of trends within science.

Nevertheless, few within the scientific community have been persuaded by his dreams of immortality. The Bible says it is appointed to everyone to die once (Heb. 9:27), and nothing medical science has yet uncovered has given anyone a reason to believe this will ever change. Even so, Ray Kurzweil is correct when he says death is a tragedy that rids the world of its most tested and experienced members, people whose contributions to the human race would only multiply with agelessness. Only our time on earth is limited, not our potential to touch and change the lives of those around us.

Limited Time, Unlimited Potential

People didn't always live such short lives. Prior to the global flood that nearly wiped out the human race in the days

of Noah, people routinely lived hundreds of years. Methuselah, the oldest man to ever live, didn't die until the ripe
old age of 969. After the Flood, life spans became shorter
and shorter, limiting both the time and the impact any one
human life could have on this earth. Paleontologist Kurt Wise
believes the change in life spans came as a result of a genetic
change God triggered in human beings after the Flood. This
change stopped our cells from continually replacing cells
that die, so our tissues began to degenerate and our bodies to
age.[1] By doing so, God purposely limited the time individuals would be able to live. Why would He do such a thing?
God wasn't being cruel. Instead, He shortened our life spans
to protect us from ourselves. The first eleven chapters of the
Bible show how humanity's potential for changing the world
is only exceeded by its potential for evil.

None of us knows how long we will live. Our time on
earth is limited. Even in the days of Methuselah, people died
unexpectedly from alligator attacks and rockslides. Each of
us must therefore choose each day how we will use the time
we have. We can use our time in a way that honors God and
yields lasting fruit—both on this earth and in eternity—or
we can (at best) waste it or (at worst) use it for evil. There
is no middle ground. Former major league outfielder Chad
Curtis put it this way: "Whatever you are doing in your life,
you are doing one of two things. You are either going up
for God or you are going down from God. One way or the
other."[2] When it comes to time, there is no middle ground.
We've been entrusted with a limited amount of time to use
for or against God.

Most of us don't want to think in such terms. We don't
want to think of our time on earth as limited, nor do we
want to feel forced to spend it in any particular way. Many

of the people I come across are more interested in just living their lives and taking things as they come, not worrying about what their lives are accomplishing. They might think reincarnation is a bunch of bunk, but they live as though they'll get a life do-over in case they don't get this one right. Rather than think long-term, they make decisions in the heat of the moment, never giving a thought to how those decisions will affect the rest of their lives.

Others live as though they have all the time in the world. They rush around like the rest of us but never get around to doing what they say is important to them. Like a child who keeps telling her parents she will clean her room soon but never does, they mean well, but their good intentions cannot overcome the immediacy of the moment. They don't seem too worried about it, though. After all, they have all the time in the world.

Borrowed Treasure

Carl Sandburg called time "the coin of your life." It is a treasure delivered to us each morning when we wake up. Imagine if one morning you stumbled over a huge bag of cash by your bed with a note attached to it. The note tells you to use the money however you want—spend it or invest it. However, any leftover cash and the items you bought that day will disappear before the next morning. The investments will last; however, the returns will all go back to the one who left the cash at the foot of your bed. Somewhere at the bottom of the note is the name of the cash's owner and his intention to talk to you someday about what you did with his money, but the pile of cash at your feet makes you skip over that part.

Overjoyed by your good fortune, you cancel whatever you had planned for the day and go out and live like a millionaire. You spend, spend, spend, and enjoy, enjoy, enjoy. After all, how often do you wake up and find a bag of cash at the foot of your bed? You eat at the best restaurants and drive the fanciest car and indulge yourself with the best of everything. Although it takes some doing, you try to spend every dime you found in the bag since none can be kept through the next day.

Sure enough, when you wake up the next morning, your leftover cash is gone along with the fancy sports car and everything else you bought the day before. You roll out of bed and start to walk toward the shower, thinking about how fun it was to live like the other half if only for one day, when you trip over another bag of cash with another note attached. The same thing happens the next day and the next and the next, until you start expecting to find a bag of cash at the foot of your bed when you wake up. Every day you do your best to spend it all as you live like a millionaire and enjoy everything you could possibly ever want.

Then one day you roll out of bed and head straight toward the spot where the bag of cash usually sits, and it isn't there. Instead you find a summons. The man whose cash you've been throwing around wants to see you. He wants to find out what you've done with his money and what you have to show for the months and months of finding a bag of cash at the foot of your bed. On your way to his house, you start preparing your speech. You plan to thank him for the cash and all the fun you had with it. But then you start to wonder what he means by asking what you have to show for the months and months of finding the cash at the foot of your bed. How can you have anything to show for it, since everything you bought along with all the leftover money disappeared when the sun came up the next morning?

That's when it hits you: you didn't have to spend all the money. You could have invested it, since the returns on the investments would last beyond one day. But you never thought about investing it since you wouldn't get to keep any of it. On your way to give an account for what you did with this guy's money, you start to wonder about your investment strategy, but of course, by then it's too late.

In a very real sense, this is the situation you and I face every day. The time we've been given is a treasure. We can spend it however we want, but we cannot save it. Time passes whether we want it to or not, and there's nothing we can do to change that fact. Nor do we ultimately get to keep anything on which we spend it. We check out of this life exactly like we walked in, empty-handed. However, we will have to answer to the One who gave us this time. The Bible says one day each one of us will stand before God and explain how and why we did what we did with the lives He gave us (2 Cor. 5:10). We won't answer only for the individual acts that filled our days; we will also have to explain our investment strategy for our lifetimes, telling God why we used the life He gave us as we did.

Thinking of time as a treasure entrusted to us changes our perspective completely. It leaves us more introspective, more discerning of how we spend it. Thinking in these terms doesn't come naturally. In *Tuesdays with Morrie*, the character Morrie Schwartz says, "We're so wrapped up with egotistical things, career, family, having enough money, meeting the mortgage, getting a new car, fixing the radiator when it breaks—we're involved in trillions of little acts just to keep going. So we don't get into the habit of standing back and looking at our lives and saying, Is this all? Is this all I want? Is something missing?"[3]

These questions should constantly run through our minds. Time can only be spent, never saved. We should then ask ourselves every day, *How am I spending the treasure God has entrusted to me?*

First Things First

If Ray Kurzweil's prediction of future immortality ever came true, perhaps we wouldn't have to be so careful how we spend the limited time we've been given. But it won't and we do. To make matters worse, there is no shortage of those eager to help us spend the limited time resources we have. More often than not, these people don't come across as sinister time thieves intent on wasting our lives by encouraging us to spend eight hours to break our son's high score on *Gran Turismo 4.* Instead they wear labels like *career advancement,* and *but I really want to do this, Mom,* and *an opportunity like this doesn't come around every day.* Trying to figure out the best way to invest time can be very confusing. We're surrounded by so many choices of things that appear to be good that we can often lose sight of what is worthy of a lifetime investment.

Influencing lives and storing up treasure in heaven take time. Lots and lots of time. Along the way we often see little if any progress. By faith we trust God meant what He said about our lives counting for eternity when we put His kingdom first. Living for delayed rewards makes us especially vulnerable to time choices that offer immediate payoffs. God never sends out a monthly statement from the First Bank of Heaven to tell us how much we have invested up there. Nor do we often have someone come alongside us and say, "You've changed my life."

However, you can see the results of a promotion at work, even though it takes time away from your family and church. Transformed attitudes and changed values in the lives you've touched are hard to gauge, but you can tally sales figures and units constructed. That's why the things of this world can so easily entangle us. They give us a sense that we're actually accomplishing something with our lives. Using time wisely means saying no to immediate gratification and choosing a sacrificial path of devoting ourselves to what matters most.

Writing these words is easy for me, but Jim had to live them out. An engineer with a major chemical company, his career was on the fast track to success. Young, bright, and energetic, he had everything necessary to quickly ascend the corporate ladder. The promotions started coming early on. By the time he'd been on the job four years, he'd already moved past people who'd worked at the company much longer. Jim and his wife, Gail, enjoyed the perks his job gave along with the added benefits of being a two-income, professional couple. They bought a nice house in suburban Chicago along with a boat and all the other toys upwardly mobile couples buy. The pace hardly slowed after their first child came along. Gail dropped Hannah off at day care on her way into work, and Jim picked her up on his way home.

Everything changed after the birth of Jim and Gail's second daughter. Alexis arrived a few weeks premature, and while she didn't have any life-threatening complications, she required the kind of care not offered in a day-care center. Gail used all her paid maternity leave plus six weeks of unpaid leave. When it came time for her to return to work, Jim used his remaining vacation time to stay home with Alexis, then put in for six weeks of paternity leave to stretch his time with her even further. He didn't think the leave would be a problem; after all, he wasn't asking for the time off with pay. But when he returned to work, he discovered putting his family before his job was tantamount to career suicide.

He was demoted during his absence. Someone else took his place as the rising golden boy of the company. Less than a month after returning to a smaller office, diminished responsibilities, and a pay cut, Jim made a radical decision he and Gail never regretted. He walked away from his career to become a stay-at-home dad. The choice came with a price. The house shrunk, the toys disappeared, and Jim saw fewer tangible signs that he was accomplishing anything with his life. But to Jim, saying no to a job that demanded his all was worth it to say yes to something that would last much longer. Jim knew his time with his daughters was limited. He faced the same choice we all must make. We've been entrusted with a treasure we can spend or invest, but we cannot save. How we use it is completely up to us, but the ramifications of our decision will last forever. Time is the coin of your life. How will you spend it?

Chapter 11

In the Moment

In the external scheme of things,
this evening is as brief as the twinkling of an eye,
yet such twinklings are what eternity is made of.

FRED ROGERS

##

To enjoy your work and accept your lot
in life—that is indeed a gift from God. People
who do this rarely look with sorrow on the past,
for God has given them reasons for joy.

ECCLESIASTES 5:19–20 (NLT)

*F*or years the future held my mind hostage. I couldn't get away from thinking about new goals and the next great challenge I wanted to tackle as soon as I'd finished wrestling with today's great challenge. I've always been a dreamer and a planner, but through most of my twenties and thirties, those dreams and plans had such a hold on my imagination that I always rushed through today to get to tomorrow. Back then I wouldn't have even read a book like this, much less attempted to write one, because I thought my system worked perfectly. Who has time to contemplate a silly question like, *How small does my life need to be to matter?* in the middle of setting and chasing goals, each one bigger than the last? I didn't. The future had me in its grasp, and I loved it. I wondered why everyone didn't live my way.

Then one day the wheels started coming off my goals and dreams. I left a growing church in California to become the pastor of a church in a small Indiana town. Of course, I took my bag of dreams with me. In five years the California church I served in a tiny community in the foothills of the Sierra Nevada Mountains had more than quadrupled in size and made a major impact on the town. One Easter nearly one in six people in the area came to our church's services. I expected to see the same thing happen in Indiana, but in a much shorter amount of time. After all, now I knew what to do.

But as you might guess since I'm writing about it, none of the dreams I had for my new church happened. Instead I found myself in the middle of a spiritual mess that had been spoiling the Indiana church for more than twenty-five years. In 1972 the church fired a pastor for the first time, and since then no pastor had survived more than five years on the job. Those who weren't dismissed recognized the writing on the wall and got out of Dodge.

Many people in the congregation didn't like how their pastors were treated, which caused a split, followed by a reconciliation a year or two later, only to be followed by a second split when another pastor was fired. The final split remains to this day. One former pastor suffered a nervous breakdown as a result of his experience in this church. Another had to plead with the finance committee chairman to stop withholding his paychecks so he could feed his wife and four children while he waited for his missionary appointment to the Philippines to go through.

I didn't know any of this until the middle of my fifth year in the church. By then it was my turn to be shown the door by the same group of people who'd made running off pastors into an art form. They made my life miserable for two years, hoping I would get the hint and leave. Finally, when I wouldn't, they demanded my resignation. My crime? I wouldn't preach against people wearing shorts. The story had a happy ending, sort of. I didn't quit and the cycle of pastoral abuse was stopped once and for all. But I never saw my goals for the church come to fruition. Apparently that wasn't God's plan for me in that church.

When the future looks bright and goals are being met, thinking about tomorrow is a joy. But when the future turns into a dark and stormy place you want no part of, simply getting out of bed in the morning takes all the energy you can muster. I know that from experience. During two years of fighting to keep my head above water, I stopped living in tomorrow. God taught me to stop and experience the present moment. My job stunk. I hated thinking about work when I went home from the office, so I didn't. Instead I focused on being completely present with my wife and children.

At the time this family focus was merely a defense mechanism that allowed me to keep my sanity, but it didn't take long for me to realize that God was teaching me a lesson I should have learned years earlier. Life's moments pass too quickly. Instead of brushing past them as though they were strangers in a crowd on our way to what we really want out of life, we need to embrace them, experience them, and allow God to use us in the moment in which we find ourselves. When we do, we find that order replaces our usual chaos and that our lives will start rubbing off on the lives of others. Living in the moment allows our lives to matter.

The Gift of Presence

Living in the moment almost sounds like some esoteric, mystical, out-of-body experience, as if you should dim the lights and plug in a CD of Benedictine monks chanting while reading the chapter. But the concept is much more down to earth. Immersing ourselves in the moment simply means focusing our attention on the people and events around us, rather than letting our thoughts rush ahead to the future or having them lag behind in the past. When we carry on a conversation with someone, living in the moment means listening to what they have to say rather than thinking of what you want to say next. We make ourselves completely there with those around us.

When my oldest daughter went off to college, she chose a school three and one-half hours from home. Freshmen were not allowed to have cars on campus, which didn't matter since we didn't have an extra car to send with her anyway. All of this meant that whenever she came home for a weekend, someone in the family would have to drive three and one-half hours west, spend all of ten minutes in Decatur, Illinois, loading my daughter, her books, and her laundry into the car, only to turn around and drive another three and one-half hours east to our home in Indiana. A couple of days later we would reload the car and take her back to school.

Because of our work schedules, and the prospect of spending fourteen hours in the car over a weekend, my wife and I would alternate. One of us would pick our daughter up and the other would take her back. Even so, these weekends meant a lot of driving, at least half of it alone in the car. I don't know about you, but I can think of plenty of things I would rather be doing than driving up and down the interstate system in the Midwest. You can stare out the windows at corn and soybean fields for only so long, and even those look better than three and one-half hours of darkness. Driving down the interstate at night is like being stuck on a treadmill. The scenery never really changes. The blacktop illuminated by the headlights looks the same no matter what state you are in.

About ten minutes into the drive home with my daughter, I realized neither the distance nor the time in the car mattered. The drive was still long and the cornfields didn't get more exciting. The change took place inside the car as a long drive was transformed into quality father-daughter time. The two of us talked all the way from Decatur to Indianapolis. We talked about her school and music and recited lines from our favorite lame movies. I could have easily sat there thinking about all I would be doing if I weren't stuck behind the steering wheel of a car. Instead, I embraced this moment God gave the two of us and enjoyed the presence of my daughter for three and one-half uninterrupted hours.

God places people around us for a reason. He doesn't want us to withdraw into ourselves or create distance even as we're sitting in the same room. Living in the moment means opening up our eyes to those around us—friends, family, and even strangers. See them for who they truly are and enjoy their presence. Learn from them. Laugh with them. Be fully present with them. These are the moments when our lives are most likely to rub off on one another—something that won't happen if we see people as projects or cast off their thoughts as nothing more than filler to keep the conversation going. Immersing ourselves in the moment means showing people how important they are to us by giving them the gift of our full attention.

Living in the Now

Living in the moment also means embracing our current circumstances and learning to enjoy our lives as they are right now, rather than thinking only of what might have been or what may be. King Solomon said it best: "I have seen that there is nothing better than for a person to enjoy his activities, because that is his reward" (Eccles. 3:22). Too few of us have discovered this reward. Instead we approach life like I approach the car radio. My favorite station is the Scan button. As Jerry Seinfeld once said, "I'm not interested in what is on the radio. I'm interested in what *else* might be on the radio."

That's how most of us live our lives—always thinking about everything *else* we need to be doing or the places we would rather be instead of focusing on the moment we are in right now. Hitting the Scan button on life keeps us from finding peace or joy. Instead, the constant search for the place we would rather be fills our lives with an ever-increasing amount of activity and frustration. Living in the moment means making a conscious decision to quiet our thoughts and fully experience the moment in which we find now ourselves.

These moments don't have to be anything grand or special. You don't have to get away to some dream location to learn to enjoy the moment. In fact, unless you learn to be in the now while sitting on a porch swing with your wife or walking up a fairway with a friend, you will not be able to fully experience the dream places you've always wanted to visit. The important thing is not where you are but being completely present wherever you may be.

Learning to enjoy the moment is a gift from God, a sort of oasis in the midst of a dry, draining world. When we pull back from the rush to get on to life's next destination, we're able to recognize God's hand at work around us. Such moments leave us thanking God as He allows us to see how truly blessed we are, even when life isn't going the way we would like it to.

When Life Spins out of Control

Talking about living in the moment sounds great when life is pleasant, but when hard times strike, we prefer to get past them as quickly as possible. During the two years of pastoral torture I endured, I constantly dreamed of leaving that place. I interviewed for a writing job in Atlanta and danced all the way to the airport, thinking I had it. On the flight back to Indianapolis, I tried to come up with the perfect way to say those two little words I'd wanted to say for a very long time: "I quit!" But I didn't get the job, and the pressure kept mounting in my church. I felt like a failure because I couldn't turn the situation around. All I really wanted was out.

God not only wouldn't let me out, He forced me to live in the moment I wanted to run away from. He had a plan, although I didn't care for it at the time. Through this time of misery, the Lord wanted me to experience His faithfulness to His promises firsthand. He also wanted to show me how He could answer prayer and work through a situation, even when nothing turned out the way I hoped. I discovered He is still faithful even when my worst-case scenarios came true.

I'm not sure when the apostle Paul experienced this truth for the first time, but it was long before he embarked on his fourth missionary journey. This wasn't the ordinary missionary endeavor, since Paul didn't choose where he would go or how long he would stay. His journey began when a group of incensed city dwellers dragged him from the temple to beat him to death. Some Roman soldiers stepped in and saved his life, but they didn't let him go. They arrested him even though they didn't know if he'd committed a crime. Paul's life went downhill from there. By the time his "journey" came to an end, he'd been locked up for three years, was nearly killed at sea, and survived a shipwreck, beatings, and a poisonous snakebite (see Acts 21–28).

Reading through the biblical account of Paul's travails on his trip in chains from Jerusalem to Rome, I'm struck by the fact that Paul never complains. At one point he is locked up and forgotten in a Caesarean jail for a year and a half. Paul obviously had better things to do with his time than to rot away in a jail cell. After all, God had laid on him the task of taking the good news of Jesus to the Roman Empire. He had books of the Bible to write, leaders to train, and false prophets to confront. Even if he didn't need to do any of those things, anything would have been a better use of his time. He lost control of his life for three years, yet he never complained. Not once did Paul waver from his conviction that God was in control of his circumstances.

Paul shows us what it means to live in the moment, even when the moment in which you find yourself leaves something to be desired. The decision to accept your present fate as God's will isn't just a decision to stop obsessing over tomorrow. Living in the now means entrusting your life to God one moment at a time. We don't know what tomorrow may hold. We don't know if we will even have a tomorrow. But if we cannot trust God with this present moment, what exactly does our faith mean?

This is the decision we face every moment of every day. Not only must we use our time wisely, but we must also trust God enough to accept the moment we are in—good times or bad—as His will for our lives. When we choose to accept this moment as God's will for our lives, we can then look for opportunities to be used by Him within it. Living in the moment means meeting God in every moment of our lives and fully experiencing anything and everything He has for us there.

Chapter 12

Holy Interruptions

It is part of the discipline of humility . . .
that we do not assume that our schedule is our own
to manage, but allow it to be arranged by God.

DIETRICH BONHOEFFER, *LIFE TOGETHER*

‖‖‖‖‖‖‖‖‖‖‖‖‖‖‖‖‖‖‖‖‖‖‖‖‖‖‖‖‖‖‖‖‖‖‖‖‖‖‖

A man's heart plans his way,
but the Lord determines his steps.

PROVERBS 16:9

*T*ime, like money, should always be held loosely. That way it doesn't hurt as much when God yanks it out of our hands. And He will yank it away. We do not know what tomorrow may hold; all of our careful planning collapses in a heap when God decides to let life throw us a curve.

You've had those days that start off like any other day, but somewhere between pouring milk on your Wheaties and your second cup of coffee, one of your children walks into the kitchen with an announcement that alters the rest of your day, if not your week. The hitch doesn't have to be overly dramatic. Most come as a series of small, unplanned diversions that make your day turn out completely different than you'd anticipated when you crawled out of bed.

Not only are these curves a part of life on planet Earth, learning to accept them is a key element of finding joy in life among the speed and distractions that so often consume us. We tend to overschedule and overcommit. Almost every minute of every day is accounted for, and those few free moments at the end of the day usually find us crashing on the sofa before the late local news comes on the air. To the carefully planned schedule, interruptions are little more than stress inducers that make life even more complicated. However, the Bible says that every time we punch an appointment into our PDAs or commit ourselves to a deadline, we must always leave room for the Lord to come in and change our plans. James 4:13–16 says, "Come now, you who say, 'Today or tomorrow we will travel to such and such a city and spend a year there and do business and make a profit.' You don't even know what tomorrow will bring—what your life will be! For you are a bit of smoke that appears for a little while, then vanishes. Instead, you should say, 'If the Lord wills, we will live and do this or that.' But as it is, you boast in your arrogance. All such boasting is evil."

James doesn't mean that every unexpected event in our day comes from God. Some interruptions are, to be sure, time thieves whose sole purpose is to pull us away from what we need to do. My sixteen-year-old daughter calls this getting distracted by something shiny. It happens to her quite frequently when she is supposed to do something she really doesn't want to do, like clean her room or empty the dishwasher. Not many sixteen-year-olds like to clean their rooms or empty the dishwasher. I'm in my midforties and I don't like doing them.

Shiny things pull us away from needed tasks and leave us sitting on the couch, watching *Rambo* movie marathons instead of finishing that project our wives asked us to do a month ago. Overcoming the lure of the shiny requires a great deal of self-discipline and prayer. I often start my workday with the prayer, "Lord, protect me from shiny things."

However, not every interruption should be ignored. God often comes along with holy interruptions designed to pull us out of the ordinary and into His extraordinary. Unfortunately, these don't come with neon signs announcing His intentions. If we aren't careful, we can miss them completely, especially when we get zealous about making every minute count. Some of God's best interruptions can appear to be colossal wastes of time. They don't always result in some profound change in another person's life or a keen insight into God's character, but that doesn't make them any less holy. Rather than fight every unscheduled surprise in our day, we need to learn to recognize God's hand in everything that comes our way and respond accordingly. Life is much more fun when we give God a free hand to redirect our steps without demanding that He explain Himself first.

Go Lie Down under the Stars

When God made the universe, He filled it with breathtaking beauty. He didn't have to. Nothing within the inner workings of nature demands that the clouds lift off of the Sierra Nevada Mountains right before the sun goes down on a winter day, causing the snowcapped peaks to almost look aflame from the orange rays of the sun. Nor did He have to create the incredible variety of wildflowers that turn the side of a Texas highway into an artist's canvas every spring. God did it because He wanted to. No one twisted His arm to make the sight of storm clouds moving across the water at

Cape Cod a wonder to behold, nor did someone else suggest He make the sight of the sun dancing off of a trout hiding under the surface of a mountain stream so incredible. The great Artist simply decided to take out His brushes on the six days He spoke all of creation into existence and create a masterpiece the human race would spend their entire existence trying to match. He didn't make the physical universe simply useful; He made it beautiful.

Why would God do such a thing? He did it because it brought Him pleasure, just as it now brings Him pleasure to see us enjoy His handiwork. From time to time He stops us in our tracks to let us do just that. We will be going along in the usual flow of life, oblivious to everything except the appointment we're already late for, when God grabs our attention with a double rainbow out the window. My favorite moment like this came one Friday while my wife and I were having lunch with some friends in a restaurant in Pismo Beach, California. I happened to glance out the window and saw a large splash far out in the water. Only one thing I knew of could displace that much water. We found some binoculars, went to a cliff overlooking the ocean, and spent the next few hours watching humpback whales play in the water. I didn't accomplish anything that afternoon, but all four of us walked away in awe of God.

When we take time to notice, God's artistry always leaves us praising Him. In Psalm 8:3–4 David wrote, "When I observe Your heavens, the work of Your fingers, the moon and the stars, which You set in place, what is man that You remember him, the son of man that You look after him?" I think these words came after David spent the night lying under the sky, watching for falling stars and feeling the awe that comes from the sight of a night sky in an arid environment free of light pollution. David had battles to fight and a people to rule, but God put all that on hold long enough to let him feel the awe and wonder that comes from the beauty of creation.

The Lord does the same for us when we allow the rush of life to so consume us that we stop seeing God's presence in our daily lives. He made this earth for us to enjoy, not just for us to use. Why else would there be such beauty in it? You need God to disrupt your schedule so that you spend time driving down the Pacific Coast Highway or stand under the stars in the mountains above Santa Fe. Take time to sit on the beach at Cape Cod and watch the surf crash in or stand in a field and watch the sky explode with color as the sun sets over an Indiana farm on a clear winter day. Let God interrupt your day and remind you of how glorious He truly is as you gaze on the wonder of His handiwork.

Go Take a Nap

God doesn't want us to go, go, go twenty-four hours a day, seven days a week. He didn't make our bodies for that kind of pace. Our bodies need rest or they will stop working properly. Sometimes we forget that God Himself took a day off after He created the universe in six days. He didn't need to rest; speaking the world into existence didn't wear Him out. Instead, God rested on the seventh day as a gift to us. Six days are enough to accomplish everything we need to get done in a week. He set aside the seventh day as a time of rest in which our minds and bodies can be rejuvenated. Just in case we missed His point, God included the Sabbath in the Ten Commandments. In between "Do not misuse the name of the Lord your God," and "Honor your father and your mother," God orders us to take a day off.

Of course, that doesn't mean we will listen. Preferring to burn out rather than rust out, we keep pushing and doing more and more. We might take a day off from our jobs, but that doesn't mean we rest. Between projects around the house and playing as hard as we can with our friends, we go back to work on Mondays more exhausted than we left. That's when God steps in and forces us to do that which we will not do voluntarily. He interrupts our busy schedules to force us to go take a nap.

Elijah was a great prophet in the Old Testament who stood up to both kings and rulers for His God. One of the my favorite stories in all the Bible is found in 1 Kings 18, where Elijah has a showdown with 850 false prophets to determine once and for all which god is real. The 850 false prophets had the support of the king and his wife, but Elijah had the Lord on his side.

The contest rules were simple. Whoever could get their god to rain down fire from the sky won. Elijah let the other side go first. The 850 prophets danced around all day, chanting and singing and crying out to their god Baal. Eventually they resorted to cutting themselves to show their sincerity. Once they all fell to the ground exhausted, Elijah stepped up. He made an altar out of twelve stones, one for each of the twelve tribes of Israel, laid some wood and a bull on the altar, then drenched the thing in water. Instead of putting on a religious show, he simply prayed and God responded. Fire fell from heaven and consumed the bull, the wood, even the stones of the altar.

This should have been the high point of Elijah's life, but it wasn't. He followed up his victory by running all the way to the capitol city for a little showdown with the king and his wicked queen, a woman named Jezebel. His showdown and the subsequent marathon left him exhausted, both emotionally and physically. The man who single-handedly took on 850 false prophets ended up in the middle of the desert, asking God to kill him because his life was a failure.

God responded in a curious way. He made Elijah go to sleep. We don't know how long Elijah slept, but the Bible indicates it was a long time. At the end of his nap God woke Elijah and surprised him with some bread and a jug of water. Keep in mind, Elijah was alone in the middle of nowhere. Then after eating all he wanted, Elijah fell back asleep. Only after his final nap was Elijah ready for God's next assignment.

When we ignore God's command to rest, He will, by His grace, force us to do what we will not do on our own. Often this comes in the form of an illness that leaves us in bed, unable to do anything but sleep. At other times He lets a winter storm shut down the city and our lives, so we have no choice but to do nothing at all except play Monopoly with our kids for a couple of days. We usually moan and complain about how much we need to do and how we don't have time to sit around doing nothing. Instead we need to accept God's gift of rest. If the Lord of the universe took a day off even though He had a universe to run, how much more so should we?

Now?

God doesn't just interrupt our lives when we are busy. "If the Lord wills, we will live and do this or that" (James 4:15) doesn't just apply to our plans for working and making money. We must take the same approach to our long-term goals for retirement. God's plans for your life and mine don't end when we turn sixty-five. In fact, the day we retire from our day jobs may be the day God's plan for our lives is just getting started.

God called Moses to be the savior of His people when Moses was well past a normal retirement age. Charlton Heston may have been in his early thirties when he walked up to the burning bush, but the real Moses was eighty. That's right—eighty. At an age when Moses probably thought he would spend most of his time sitting around his tent counting his sheep, God told him to go and confront the king of the most powerful nation on earth. I'm sure there were Israelites who wondered why they should follow this geezer who had the nerve to call himself their deliverer. They might have worried about Moses' age, but God never did. He caused Moses to accomplish far more in the last forty years of his life than he did in his first eighty. Only God could do something like that.

The plans God has for your life and mine do not have an expiration date on them. He can and will completely redirect the course of our lives no matter how old or young we may be. Waiting until we're eighty isn't usually His method of operation, but the change He makes in the career paths we carefully choose can be just as dramatic. Of course, He has that right. He is, after all, the Lord of the universe. When He interrupts the life we've carefully planned for ourselves, He isn't being cruel. Instead He wants to lead you into an adventure of faith unlike anything you've ever experienced before. Paul said, "For we are His creation—created in Christ Jesus for good works, which God prepared ahead of time so that we should walk in them" (Eph. 2:10).

Planned Interruptions

You and I were created to share our lives with the God who made us. That's the primary reason we exist. God made us to know Him personally and intimately. The relationship for which He designed us was never meant to be experienced at a distance. Nor can it be watered down to religious ceremony and formulas. People try, and many of us settle for the watered-down spirituality ceremony and formulas, never knowing God offers us infinite joy in His presence. But our hearts ache for something more. You already know you were created to live in eternity even though you are now trapped in time. Yet the longing for the eternal deep inside our souls is a hunger for more than something that will outlast us. Our spirits long to know God, and until they are satisfied, our lives will never be complete.

Because we were made to know God, we need to schedule a planned interruption in our day to spend time with Him. That's easier said than done. We have a way of avoiding God. Because of our fallen condition, we usually run away from the One for whom we were made and into the arms of about anything else (Rom. 3:9–18).

The Bible says that in our natural state, none of us will seek God. We're too busy looking for God substitutes. In the Old Testament people regularly worshiped substitute gods made out of gold and silver. One of their favorites looked like a cow. I can't imagine anyone falling on his face in front of a cow, but I have been in a stadium filled with tens of thousands of screaming fanatics, all paying homage to Colts or Cowboys or, in my hometown in Oklahoma, Sooners. Who in their right mind would devote their lives to serving a statue sitting in the middle of a man-made shrine? But I've seen people turn their cars or children or, more often than not, themselves, into their own personal gods.

We weren't made to devote all our time and energy to anything that can be found in this world. We were made for eternity, not just so we could exist forever, but that we might carry on an eternal love affair with the God who created us. The craving for the eternal deep inside our souls aches for God. We're not just homesick. We are, in the truest sense of the word, lovesick. Our spirit aches to be reunited with the Supreme Lover of our souls, whether we realize it or not. Becoming a Christian and regularly attending worship services don't completely satisfy this longing. The human soul requires time to simply sit and be quiet before the God who loved us enough to sacrifice His Son on our behalf.

In Psalm 46:10 the Lord tells us to "be still, and know that I am God" (NIV). If that is what we were made for—and we were—you would think obeying this verse would be easy. But it isn't. Feel free to insert all sorts of clichés and stories about how fast life is today and how our hectic schedules crowd out time for the Lord. Let's all collectively point the finger at the postmodern world and blame it for our inability to settle down and sit silently before our God. It's a great excuse. Most of us have used it at one time or another when we feel guilty about our spiritual lives. Unfortunately, it doesn't hold water. The pace of life in the twenty-first century doesn't keep us from being quiet before God. We do.

Our souls long for God, but our minds go out of our way to avoid Him. Something about standing in front of the One who sees past all of our masks and isn't fooled by our God-talk frightens us. He leaves us feeling out of control and very, very vulnerable. Drawing near to Him makes us hyperaware of our own failures and sinfulness. As Hebrews 4:13 says, "No creature is hidden from Him, but all things are naked and exposed to the eyes of Him to whom we must give an account."

The prophet Isaiah felt this nakedness when he found himself in God's presence. He slapped his hand over his mouth and cried out, "Woe is me, for I am ruined, because I am a man of unclean lips and live among a people of unclean lips, [and] because my eyes have seen the King, the Lord of Hosts" (Isa. 6:5).

When Simon Peter first realized who Jesus was, he fell on his knees before him and said, "Go away from me, because I'm a sinful man, Lord!" (Luke 5:8). Even John, one of Jesus' closest disciples, fell at His feet like a dead man when he encountered Jesus after His resurrection (Rev. 1:17). I don't know about you, but I don't think any of these experiences sound particularly pleasant.

That's why we pull back from God even though we were made for fellowship with Him. We try not to. We pray and even read our Bibles occasionally, but it doesn't take much to keep us from making any effort at all. In some ways, the flurry of activities that we say keeps us from having a strong relationship with the Lord comes as a bit of a relief. It gives us an out. That is why we must stop running away from God and cancel all of our excuses. We must make time to be quiet before God our first priority. We can't avoid Him forever. God Himself pursues us and He will not stop until He has us. Jesus said, "You did not choose me, but I chose you" (John 15:16). He loved us first, and He keeps working in our lives to draw us to Himself so we can love Him back (1 John 4:19). Making this practice a daily reality won't be easy, but then again, since when was anything worthwhile easy?

God's holy interruptions may at first feel like a bother, yet they come as gifts of His grace. Learning to recognize them will set us well on our way to overcoming the chaos that engulfs our lives. Building these interruptions into our schedules draws us even closer to fulfilling the plans He had for us when He first created us—plans He works to fulfill no matter what we may have planned.

Chapter 13

Finding Peace in the Minivan

Little League baseball is a very good thing because it keeps the parents off the streets.
YOGI BERRA

▓▓▓

Train a child in the way he should go, and when he is old he will not turn from it.
PROVERBS 22:6 (NIV)

*A*uto racing aficionados argue over which is America's premier race—NASCAR's Daytona 500 or U.S. Auto Club's Indianapolis 500. One bills itself as the Great American Race, the other is the self-proclaimed Greatest Spectacle in Racing. But every parent knows neither one can hold a candle to the race that starts every afternoon when the school bell rings. If a television network televised the event, it would go something like this:

ALLEN: Good afternoon, I'm Allen Bestwick, along with my partner Benny Parsons, bringing you the Speed Channel's exclusive coverage of the *Dodge Caravan–Ford Freestar–Insert-SUV-Name-Here After-School 500.*

BENNY: Allen, this promises to be one of the most exciting races we've covered this week. We're here at the start line in the parking lot of Everytown Elementary School, and you can already feel the tension in the air ten minutes before the bell sounds. These drivers are really keyed up for this afternoon of driving.

ALLEN: That's right, Benny. I need to remind our viewers that the drivers in the Dodge Caravan–Ford Freestar–Insert-SUV-Name-Here After-School 500 take off from a standing start, so starting position is very important. And for the seventh day in a row the purple 1999 Ford Windstar with the Goodyear 2000 steel-belted radials has snagged the pole. Our pit reporter Dave Burns is with driver Mary M. Take it away, Dave.

DAVE: Thanks, Allen. I'm standing here with Mary M., driver of the purple 1999 Ford Windstar with the Goodyear 2000 steel-belted radials. Mary, you've grabbed the pole for the seventh day in a row, somehow managing to put your Windstar at the front of the line of parents waiting to pick up their kids from school. What's your secret?

MARY M.: Well, Dave, the key is arriving early. I try to pull into the parking lot at least forty-five minutes before any of the other drivers. In fact, I knew my streak was on the line today, so I never left after dropping off my Johnny this morning.

DAVE: You mean you've been sitting in the parking lot since eight this morning?

MARY M.: That's right. The going got a little rough around noon, but I managed to pull through it thanks to a Snickers. Not going anywhere for awhile? Grab a Snickers. Snickers, the cure for common hunger.

DAVE: Back to you, Allen.

ALLEN: Benny, I think I see some of the other drivers complaining about Mary M. and her Windstar and her Snickers bars. Snickers, it's packed with peanuts.

BENNY: Well, Allen, any of our competitors today could spend their day in the parking lot. They're just not as committed to winning as Mary M.

Bell rings.

BENNY: Allen, the bell just sounded and our line of drivers all simultaneously fired up those roaring V-6s in their assorted minivans and SUVs. But remember, viewers at home, the race cannot begin until the school buses leave the parking lot.

ALLEN: A flood of children are now running out of the school toward the line of our parent competitors in the Dodge Caravan–Ford Freestar–Insert-SUV-Name-Here After-School 500. This is the tricky part of the race, pulling the kids into the minivans and SUVs and getting them buckled in without losing too much ground to the minivans and SUVs in front of them.

BENNY: The first bus just began to move, but there's trouble with the purple 1999 Ford Windstar. After moving just three feet the minivan slammed to a stop and an eight-year-old just sprinted out the sliding door and back into the school. Dave, can you tell us what's going on down there?

DAVE: Benny, apparently Johnny forgot his homework. This will definitely push the purple van to the back of the pack on the next leg of the race, the Junior-Senior High Oval Pickup.

ALLEN: Benny, a red 2000 Dodge Durango with Michelin All-Terrain radials just made an incredible sliding pass, pulling around the purple van. That move opened up the flow of traffic out of the parking lot.

BENNY: Allen, you know this start is so critical to the rest of the race. I talked with Dinah J., driver of the red 2000 Dodge Durango before the bell sounded. She has exactly 3.8 minutes to get from here to the high school where she will pick up her other two kids. Then she'll have only 8.2 minutes to get them to soccer practice. From there she has to drive ten miles to the east side of Bigcity for piano lessons, then back to Everytown for gymnastics, then it's back to the high school gymnasium for a volleyball game at 7:00 tonight. Finally, at 8:45, she has to get over to the Everytown park for a coed softball game. If she loses even a few seconds here to the purple van, the results could be disastrous.

ALLEN: Wow, it sounds like Dinah J. has an easier schedule than most of our competitors. Joan Z. in the green 2001 Plymouth Voyager with some off-brand tire her husband picked up at the Tire Barn—Tire Barn, for all your automotive needs: Next time you think tires, think Tire Barn—has four practices and three ball games between her three children tonight.

BENNY: And it's a good thing too, Allen. If these parents didn't run themselves ragged trying to expose their children to every possible experience under the sun, we wouldn't have a race to cover. And what a race it is. It looks like Johnny has just made it back to the purple van, but not before Mary M. falls back into twentieth position behind the tan 1996 Ford Windstar. . . .

I know this race well because I used to drive in it every afternoon. Driving the family minivan in the After-School 500 is one of the perks of being self-employed and working out of my home. I've experienced the thrill of leaving the house a few minutes before the bell rings at my daughters' school and not getting home to stay until after dark. My wife and I both know the frustration of feeling like half of our lives are spent behind the wheel of the car, running back and forth between practices and lessons and everything else our kids could become involved in. I've killed time in music stores waiting for guitar lessons to end and nearly fallen asleep in the bleachers of an old gym while the coach runs the team through just one more set of drills before letting them go home.

Through the years I even played the role of that coach nine or ten times with my girls' softball teams. My wife and I have spent many, many hours in the bleachers, watching track meets and softball games. And we've logged our share of time in folding metal chairs, attending plays, band and choir concerts, and musicals in the old high school's fabulous cafegymatorium. The town built a new school with an actual auditorium with padded theater seats, which I'm sure we will get to break in as well.

I write all of this to assure you that I am just like every parent reading this book. You may have picked this book up to bring some order to the chaotic life that accompanies raising children, but all this talk of using time like a treasure and opening your life to God's holy interruptions doesn't answer the question that runs through every minute of your days: How can I stop being a chauffeur and activity coordinator and get back to being a parent? Simplifying life sounds like a great idea, but when your children get old enough to start playing youth sports and participating in extracurricular activities, your life is suddenly filled with people who seem intent on making your life as complicated as humanly possible. Is there a way out?

A certain amount of chaos will always be a part of parenting, but there is a way to keep the chaos from consuming your life and robbing you of quality family time. To pull it off, you will need wisdom, discipline, and the willingness to utter that word children hate and parents fear: no. Above all, you need a clear sense of purpose, always keeping in mind why God entrusted children to your care.

Keep First Things First

It is easy to get confused as to what we need to accomplish in the lives of our children. More than anything, our goal should be to develop godly character. We want to instill in them things like honesty, integrity, and the value of self-sacrifice. If we aren't careful, we can easily get sidetracked and think that our job is to give our children every opportunity we didn't have growing up. That is how we end up spending half our day behind the wheel of a minivan, running back and forth between school and lessons and practices. In our quest to give our children the best, we lose sight of what they need most.

Back in the Dark Ages when I was a kid, the Olympic games were cast as a showdown between the forces of good, the United States and our allies, against the forces of evil, the Soviet Union and its satellite states. Whoever won the most medals somehow took the lead in the cold war and proved it gave its people a better way of life. Back then stories surfaced of Communist bloc Olympic factories where children were taken from their families at a young age, so that they could devote themselves morning, noon, and night to gymnastics or diving or team handball or whatever sport was the cold war showdown du jour.

Here in the U. S. of A., we took pride in the fact that our athletes were allowed to live normal lives while excelling on the field of play. But that is no longer the case. I recently read of a young American Olympic champion whose success came as a result of leaving home at the age of eleven to live closer to the national training center. Her mother kept an apartment near her, while her father stayed home in Minnesota or North Dakota or somewhere cold to keep the family business going, so that he could afford the high price of making his daughter an Olympic champion. He rarely saw her, and the two never spent anytime together. She won the gold medal, but at what cost?

I know most of us will never face such a choice, but even in the small town where I live, parents find themselves pressured to spend all of their time and energy, not to mention a good deal of their money, on their child's athletic career. Families lose mealtimes together around the table and instead wolf down fast food in the car on their way to the nightly three-hour gymnastics sessions or basketball practices or cheerleading or whatever sport is popular that day. For what? Sports may be a great way to learn lessons for life, but we live in an obsessive culture that quickly loses perspective on the whats and whys of life. The only way to resist their pull is to focus on what matters most in the life of your child and not let anything get in the way of it.

Limit the Chaos

Involving our children in music, sports, band, speech, or any other options available through schools and other organizations is a good thing. Overinvolvement is not. Knowing where to draw the line makes the difference between fruitful and frustrated. Most of us want to expose our children to a variety of experiences and allow them to experiment to find what they may be good at. Today they just *have* to take art classes; tomorrow it may be guitar lessons. Every parent has been there. This sort of smorgasbord approach to life is part of being a child. The world seems so full of possibilities. Kids want to try them all.

As parents, our job is to limit the number of possibilities our children can experience at a time. Allowing them to try a little of everything at once doesn't do either of you any favors. My wife and I told our daughters they could try whatever sports and activities they wanted; however, we limited them to one sport or activity at a time, especially when we were the ones driving them back and forth to practice.

Too many parents act as though their children will fall behind for life if they don't do extracurricular activities—that or they are just afraid to tell their kids no. Either way, they end up with a child who is on both the swim and basketball teams while also trying to work in gymnastics and dance. Why would you put yourself or them through that much frustration? Cut down on the chaos by limiting the child to one activity or the other, rather than trying to do them all. This season let them try swimming. Next season it may be basketball. Or softball. Or nothing at all. Experiment until your child finds something he or she truly enjoys.

In spite of what television commercials may say, you can't do it all. No one can. We throw our lives out of balance and out of control when we try. When we let our children try to do everything, they miss out on experiences they will never have again. Kids need time to be kids. They need time to play in the backyard or lie around doing nothing but laughing with their brothers and sisters. More than anything, they need time with you. Guard that time by cutting out simultaneous activities and sports.

Say No to Overeager Coaches and Activity Leaders

It was a tough loss, no doubt about it—the latest in a string of tough losses that pushed the coach's patience to the limit. He'd entered the season with high hopes. The team looked sharp in early workouts. A few of the players were a little green, but the coach thought he had enough experience in his lineup to more than make up for them.

Pitching, as always, was a concern, but the team's batters were lively and, aside from one outfield position, the defense looked strong. Then the regular season started and the team never lived up to its potential. They had trouble putting together consecutive innings of solid, fundamental baseball. Their decision making also left a lot to be desired.

Base-running errors drove the coach nuts, and when the center-fielder missed the cutoff man for the second time in the same inning, the coach contemplated hanging it up. His wife cooled him down when he got home, which made him decide to try one last approach.

At the end of practice one sunny Tuesday afternoon, the coach sat his team down and challenged them to raise their level of play. "I want all of you to do a gut check," he barked at them. "Each one of you has to decide if you are willing to do whatever it takes to make this team a winner."

He kept talking, but by that point most of the players had tuned him out. The second he said the words gut check, the majority of the six-year-old boys on the team started poking one another in the stomach and laughing uncontrollably. They never turned their season around, but then again, most of them didn't really care as long as they got a free soda after every game.

Coaches can easily lose perspective. I know. I coached my daughters' fast-pitch softball teams for ten years. In the heat of competition we coaches sometimes start to act as though this baseball game between a bunch of nine- and ten-year-olds is exceeded in importance only by the Super Bowl, and that only barely. That's when we begin scheduling four-to five-hour practices six and seven days a week.

Parents are even worse. The moment a child puts on a uniform, even if it is nothing more than a navy blue T-shirt with "Yankees" silk-screened across the front, a parent's eyes start to play tricks on him. He stops seeing his six-year-old son who just mastered the art of tying his own shoes last week and instead sees a young Mickey Mantle. Unless something snaps us back into reality, we will spend every moment of every day working to hone our child's latent athletic skills in preparation for his life in the major leagues. We then put the child on a traveling team, so he can play in tournaments against the best competition, even though the games tie up every weekend between May and October. Some youth baseball leagues now play nearly as many games as the pros.

Enough is enough. Just say no to overeager coaches and other activity leaders. When that gymnastics coach tells you your daughter needs to come into the Gym Nest for four hours a day five days a week, stop and listen to what she is actually telling you. Do you really want your daughter spending more time with some coach you hardly know instead of you? What benefit will she derive from giving up her childhood to perfect a balance-beam routine?

Gymnastics aren't the only sport that demands such commitment. They all do. As a parent, let me just say that this is ridiculous. The odds against your child earning a college scholarship or turning pro as a result of all the extra practices and games are astronomical. And even if they are one of the lucky ones who move on to the next level, is a few thousand dollars toward a college education really worth the loss of quality family time? No way. The time you have together as a family is severely limited. You have your children under your roof for a brief moment, and then they will be gone. Why, then, would we allow a silly game to rob us of our time and steal these moments we will never get back?

Our children grow up fast. Very fast. I always thought this was just a cliché until the day my wife and I moved one of our children into a college dorm. Make the most of the moments. Reserve time for the family. Go on vacations together even if it is just a getaway to the local lake. My dad once told me to enjoy my children. Make that your goal and keep the madness under control. It will all end very soon.

Harder

Chapter 14

Happily Ever After

*We are half-hearted creatures, fooling about
with drink and sex and ambition when infinite joy is
offered us, like an ignorant child who wants to go on
making mud pies in a slum because he cannot imagine
what is meant by the offer of a holiday at the sea.*

C. S. LEWIS, *THE WEIGHT OF GLORY*

▬▬▬▬▬▬▬▬▬▬▬▬▬▬▬▬▬▬▬▬▬▬

*Rejoice always! Pray constantly.
Give thanks in everything, for this is
God's will for you in Christ Jesus.*

1 THESSALONIANS 5:16–18

*H*e had everything. Money. Power. Fame. And women.
Lots and lots of women. He didn't have to break a
sweat for his wealth. The inheritance from his father gave
him a good start, and his head for business and a knack for
real estate did the rest. At one point his annual income hit
nine figures. As his affluence grew, so did his fame. Crowds
from around the world came to see him. He was perhaps
the first global celebrity. But he didn't just sit around making money. He invested his fortune and launched building
projects that would make Donald Trump green with envy.
In his spare time he dabbled in philosophy and wrote a

few best-sellers. And then there were the parties. He could throw a party like no one had ever seen before.

He had everything, but everything wasn't enough. As he neared the end of his life he penned these words: "I looked most carefully into everything, searched out all that is done on this earth. And let me tell you, there's not much to write home about. God hasn't made it easy for us. I've seen it all and it's nothing but smoke—smoke, and spitting into the wind. Life's a corkscrew that can't be straightened, a minus that won't add up. I said to myself, 'I know more and I'm wiser than anyone before me in Jerusalem. I've stockpiled wisdom and knowledge.' What I've finally concluded is that so-called wisdom and knowledge are mindless and witless— nothing but spitting into the wind. Much learning earns you much trouble. The more you know, the more you hurt" (Eccles. 1:13–18 MSG).

These words sound like something Ernest Hemingway might have written on the night he took his own life in July 1961. Hemingway also had everything, but he never knew true peace. He ran from one experience to another, one woman after another, but nothing satisfied him. Throughout his life he tried to eliminate even the memory of his Christian upbringing. He didn't just rebel against God and his parents, he completely discarded them. Some say his hatred for his mother consumed him, even as much as his rampant alcoholism.

But Hemingway didn't write these words. They came from the pen of a preacher, not a pagan; a man so close to God that he wrote three books of the Bible. We don't usually think of him as a skeptic. Instead, we remember him for his incredible wisdom. Solomon was wiser than anyone before or after him. He was the greatest king Israel ever knew, the wisest man to ever live, and in his masterpiece, the Book of Ecclesiastes, he was the spokesman for the postmodern age.

Solomon reached heights the rest of us can only dream about. Along the way he discovered that unlimited wealth and power aren't all they're cracked up to be. In the middle of his parties, he felt an ache in his soul for something more substantial than building projects and collecting monkeys and peacocks. By writing about his experience, he saved us the trouble of wasting our lives, aiming for less when so much more is offered to us. Solomon's quest in Ecclesiastes epitomizes C. S. Lewis's thoughts in *The Weight of Glory:* "If we consider the unblushing promises of reward and the staggering nature of the rewards promised in the Gospels, it would seem that Our Lord finds our desires not too strong, but too weak."[1]

All of the pleasures and projects about which Solomon writes turned out to be nothing but mud pies on a larger scale. We wonder why we can't have everything this world offers along with all God wants to give us. Yet asking that question only shows how far we still need to go. Choosing less is actually a choice for more, and we don't have to wait until our lives are over to enjoy it.

More of God

God wants to give us the gift of Himself, but we cannot receive it when our arms are too full of the world and all it offers. Our arms don't feel full. The load we carry feels like life. After all, we're just trying to get by. But God wants us to do more than get by. He invites us to live in His presence as we shift our focus off the temporal and set it squarely upon the eternal. Remember, our real lives are hidden with

Christ in God. This isn't just something we look forward to after we die. When you entrust your life to Jesus, your real life already dwells in heaven even as you live in the world of time.

In God's presence we find what cannot be found anywhere else. David spoke of this as he sang to the Lord, "In Your presence is abundant joy; in Your right hand are eternal pleasures" (Ps. 16:11). Just one taste and David was hooked. Never again could he be satisfied with experiencing God from afar. He wanted more and more of Him. No wonder he wrote in Psalm 63:1, "O God, You are my God; I earnestly search for You. My soul thirsts for You; my whole body longs for You in this parched and weary land where there is no water" (NLT).

We cannot experience God in this way while pursuing more stuff, more activities, and more of ourselves. It's not just that we can't; we won't. Jesus said, "No one can be a slave of two masters, since either he will hate one and love the other, or be devoted to one and despise the other" (Matt. 6:24). That doesn't stop us from trying to plug a little of God into our warp-driven, overstuffed lives, but He refuses to play that game. He loves us too much to let us think we need just enough of Him to make us feel better about ourselves at the end of a hard day. If that's all we want, we need a dog, not God.

The Lord of the universe wants us to experience life the way He meant it to be lived when He designed the human race. To do that we need to break free of the decaying world of sin and step into His eternal presence.

Once we taste more of God, we realize we didn't give up anything for Him. Paul said, " I once thought all these things were so very important, but now I consider them worthless because of what Christ has done. Yes, everything else is worthless when compared with the priceless gain of knowing Christ Jesus my Lord. I have discarded everything else, counting it all as garbage, so that I may have Christ and become one with him" (Phil. 3:7–9 NLT). Nothing compares to knowing God intimately and personally. The one thought I cannot comprehend as I contemplate all this is that God is the one who pursues this relationship with us. Jonah 2:8 says, "Those who worship false gods have turned their backs on all the mercies waiting for them from the Lord!" (TLB). God longs to pour out His mercy on us and draw us into His presence. He pursues us, we don't pursue Him (John 15:16).

Not only do we experience more of God as we drop the baggage of this temporal world, but we also see Him working in our lives in ways we never would have noticed before. Choosing a life of less means refusing to look to the things of this world for security. That leaves us with only one other option: basing our security in the Lord. David wrote in Psalm 34:5–7, "This poor man cried, and the Lord heard him and saved him from all his troubles. The angel of the Lord encamps around those who fear Him, and rescues them."

When we stop trusting in money or influence to carry us through this life, we can see the angel of the Lord doing the same thing for us. God's hand is everywhere in both the big things and the small. Watching Him work in our lives leaves us thanking Him for everything, which in turn draws us even closer to Him.

What a great bargain! Instead of walking through life with the attitude that we must own and do everything we can, we surrender all our possessions, ambitions, everything to God. Since that leaves us with nothing, we have to depend on Him for even the most basic items in life. He always comes through. But more than that, as we rely on God, we experience Him in ways we never thought possible. I think this is what Paul had in mind when he wrote, "Now to Him who is able to do above and beyond all that we ask or think—according to the power that works in you—to Him be glory in the church and in Christ Jesus to all generations, forever and ever. Amen" (Eph. 3:20–21).

More of People

God not only made us for Himself, He made us for one another. Without other people, the journey through life hardly matters. We need to connect with other human beings, to know them on a level that goes beyond, "Hey, how's it going?" Sure, we need love, but we need more than that. God designed the human soul in such a way that it must become interconnected with others in meaningful relationships. When He first created the human race, God said, "It is not good for the man to be alone" (Gen. 2:18). His statement was true then and it remains true today. Vital, growing relationships are what life is all about.

Here's the real irony: we say life is about relationships—friends and family make life worth living—and yet, people routinely sacrifice relationships in their quest to get "more out of life." The old cliché may say no one ever laid on his deathbed and wished he'd spent more time in the office, but that doesn't stop us from spending too much time there now. Parents give up time with their kids to work extra jobs to afford a larger house or a nicer car or a bass boat for the weekend.

A friend of a friend recently went through a divorce because he spent more time watching sports than he spent with his wife. When forced to choose between his college basketball season tickets and making his marriage work, he chose the former. He may be an extreme case, but his messed-up sense of priorities is growing more and more common. We live in culture that obsesses over everything except building strong, healthy relationships.

Choosing less of this world means choosing more of the only thing that lasts into the world to come: people. We can't take any of our possessions or awards or anything else with us to heaven, but we can bring other people. The influence God wants to exert through your life and mine does more than change the course of generations here on earth. When we live for eternity rather than the temporary world, we point other people toward Jesus Christ and show them what it means to know Him personally. As they follow our example and say yes to Him, both their lives today and their eternal destiny changes. We will have the privilege of spending all of eternity together with them in the presence of God.

Just imagine for a moment what this means. By putting people before possessions or prestige or any of the other temporary things this world says are important, our relationships on this earth will change dramatically. We will be set free to establish strong friendships by serving other people and considering them to be more important than ourselves. We will have time for our families, making those bonds stronger as well. Our lives will be filled with more of what we all say matters most to us.

But the payoff doesn't end there. These same relationships will then have the potential to stretch out into eternity as those we love and serve say yes to our Savior. This isn't some cheesy Hollywood movie ending where heaven is nothing more than an extended version of this earth. Instead, as we enter into the presence of God in eternity, we will thank not only our God for His grace that saved us but also those who played a role in getting us there. We truly will have more of people when we choose less of this world, both now and forever.

More of Life

Jesus said, "I came so they can have real and eternal life, more and better life than they ever dreamed of" (John 10:10 MSG). Jesus came to give us life the way God meant for it to be lived when He scooped up some dust and formed it into the first human being. Our Father never intended life on this earth to be a test of endurance. If Adam and Eve had stuck with God's original plan, no one would have ever uttered those immortal words that cross everyone's mind at some point in their lives: "Is this it?" That nagging sense of disappointment with life, that feeling that something is not quite right in the world, would not exist. Until sin entered the picture, everything was right in the world. The first man and woman lived in a paradise free of sickness, disease, disappointment, and death. More than that, they lived in perfect harmony with God.

But paradise wasn't enough for the mother and father of us all. They wanted more. They didn't want to know God; they wanted to trade places with Him. On the day they tried, God's perfect creation changed forever. When sin entered the world, death and everything it brings with it came along for the ride. The world became cursed. Incredible beauty became intertwined with suffering and pain. But that wasn't the worst of it. Human beings, creatures made to know and enjoy God, found themselves cut off from Him. A huge barrier now exists between us and God. That's why we can't walk outside and see God. Believe it or not, He did this for our own good. Anything tainted by sin cannot get near a holy God and survive the experience.

The physical world changed forever the day Adam and Eve first sinned. They wanted more and ended up with much less. Unfortunately, their descendants still haven't learned from their mistake. The world continues to perpetuate the lie that somewhere within this world of time is what we're looking for. So we go off looking for happiness in stuff or achievements or applause, but we never find the life for which we were created—that is, until we find Jesus. He came to bring us life, but this life cannot be found in anything the world has to offer. By turning from this world and entrusting our lives to Him, we reverse the curse Adam and Eve handed down to us. They wanted more and ended up with less. Now, through Christ, we choose less of this world and end up with more of the life our souls crave.

All this sounds great, but too often the picture painted of life in Christ leaves something to be desired. We hear the word Christian and immediately think of never getting to do anything more fun than sitting through some boring sermon on a hard wooden bench.

I grew up in a church tradition known for not allowing its adherents to dance. We roller-skated instead. Nor could we play cards, but we could play dominoes. By the time I came around, the rules were relaxed, but our reputation as a church where no one has fun had already been established. I laugh now as I look back on the efforts we used to make to convince our friends that you could be a Christian and still have fun. It was like a big PR campaign to try to lure skeptics into the fold.

Jesus came to give us life, and that's exactly what we experience when we move out of the world of time and begin living for eternity. Rules such as don't dance, don't play cards, don't stand on one foot while drinking orange juice (OK, I made that last one up) are little more than a ploy by the devil to cloud the issue. Colossians 2:20–23 assures us that the Christian life has nothing to do with rules. "If you died with Christ to the elemental forces of this world, why do you live as if you still belonged to the world? Why do you submit to regulations: 'Don't handle, don't taste, don't touch'? All these regulations refer to what is destroyed by being used up; they are human commands and doctrines. Although these have a reputation of wisdom by promoting ascetic practices, humility, and severe treatment of the body, they are not of any value against fleshly indulgence." Jesus didn't die so we wouldn't dance, but that we might live.

When we live for Him, we experience more of life than we ever thought possible. We're set free from the "Is this it?" syndrome and are invited to work with God in plans He made before He made the world. Ephesians 2:10 promises, "For we are God's masterpiece. He has created us anew in Christ Jesus, so that we can do the good things he planned for us long ago" (NLT). This is where real life is found. By choosing less of this world, we are able to give ourselves completely to doing the "good things" God planned for us long ago. God's plan for the human race has always revolved around undoing the damage caused by sin and restoring people to a right relationship with Him. We get to help Him do this. When we do, everything we put our hands to matters.

In Christ we are set free to be fully human for the first time in our lives. Living in Him sets our imaginations free to create, to explore, to discover the wonders of His creation. Released from the bondage of a system that says real life is measured by what we own and what we do, we are able to bring glory to God through everything we do—both large and small. And those things we do for Him matter not only in this world, but also in the world to come. Our lives aren't wasted, even if we never accomplish anything anyone would ever think of as significant. Small lives become gigantic when placed in the hands of God.

This is life. This is more. And it can only be found by choosing less.

Chapter 15

This Ain't No Doris Day Movie

If life is a bowl of cherries,
then what am I doing in the pits?
ERMA BOMBECK

▪▪▪

For which of you, wanting to build a tower,
doesn't first sit down and calculate the cost to
see if he has enough to complete it?
LUKE 14:28

Jim strolled into the kitchen, a huge grin on his face. His
wife stood next to the sink, peeling a carrot and humming
to herself. "I'm so glad we decided to simplify our lives," Jim
said to Jane. "Who knew we could be so happy? I now have so
much more time for you and our two wonderful children."

"Yes, life is wonderful," Jane replied. "We're completely
out of debt, our children never misbehave, and our relationship has never been better." She ran to Jim, threw her arms
around his neck, gazed into his eyes, and said, "I've never
loved you more. The simple life truly is the answer to all our
hopes and prayers."

"I don't know how life could get any better," Jim replied, "but I know it will. Every morning I awaken to discover even more benefits to downsizing our lives and slowing down our schedules. I only wish we'd learned the lessons earlier. We are truly living a dream."

We now interrupt this fantasy for a dose of reality: choosing to downsize and simplify will not guarantee you a trouble-free, joy-filled, wonderful life. Downsizing doesn't come with guarantees of freedom from debt, nor does it mean your children will turn out to be Nobel laureates. Don't choose this path because you think it will lead to heaven on earth. It won't. Nor should you confuse simpler with easier. Downsizing your life is not easy. Going against the conventional wisdom of a temporal world and choosing to live with an eternal focus guarantees the rest of your life will *not* be an effortless stroll to the gates of Glory.

Saying no to yourself and to the world day after day will prove to be the most difficult task you've ever attempted. Making your life small enough to matter will result in a better life; just don't expect it to be quiet and trouble free. Shortly after you start down this path, you will realize the price to be paid, and that price is not always what you might expect. Also, there are some subtle traps we must guard against, lest we get sidetracked and end up worse off than when we began.

Pride

Maybe I run in the wrong circles, but I've yet to meet anyone who finds it easy to consider other people as more important than themselves. I know a few who make this choice appear almost effortless, but looks can be deceiving.

Peyton Manning makes throwing touchdown passes look simple, but he has worked harder than almost any other quarterback in history to perfect his craft. Compared with practicing humility, Peyton's job is a piece of cake.

Since the day sin entered the world, the human heart has naturally run to put itself at the center of the universe. Maybe it's a problem of perspective. Since we experience the world through our own eyes and ears and hands, we think everyone else should see the world the same way we do. We instinctively want whatever will make life easier for the person in our skin.

A life of less begins with less of me. Before I can downsize anything else, I have to downsize my opinion of myself and choose to put others before myself. Instead of worrying about what is best for me, I must focus on what is best for others (Phil. 2). And that will not be easy. I may be able to pull it off for a day or two, but believe me, there are days when living like this is the last thing I want to do.

I've tested this humility in the hardest laboratory known to man: marriage. I've been married for more than twenty years, but even after all this time, putting my wife and children before me takes effort. Before you dismiss me as some insensitive jerk, take a good look in the mirror. Have you ever rushed to the freezer so you could get the last bite of ice cream or grumbled to yourself when your spouse asked you to get her a glass of water when you were about to crawl into bed? Of course you have. We all have. We do it because putting others first doesn't come naturally to anyone.

But that's not the worst of it. Choosing to serve other people means having to swallow our pride on a regular basis. Jesus gave us the perfect example of serving others when He washed His disciples' feet. Keep in mind, His disciples all wore sandals, most streets were dirt, and people and animals walked down the same paths. How would you like to wash *those* feet? I wouldn't. This was a job usually reserved for the lowest household servant. There's not a lot of room for pride among foot washers . . . or any other servant, for that matter. People will walk right over us and confuse our decision to humble ourselves and serve others as a sign of weakness. Most people won't applaud our efforts. Instead, they will keep right on going and never notice. The Bible says, "God resists the proud, but gives grace to the humble" (1 Pet. 5:5). Turning loose of our pride won't be easy, but it places us in the best position to have God work through us.

Boredom

Small means small. And small can mean monotony. People may wax nostalgic about going back to a simpler day where folks sat on their front porches every night, talking with family and friends, but there is a reason those days ended. The pace of postmodern life may leave us huffing and puffing, trying to catch our breath, but there is a certain excitement to the madness. Reaching deadlines, trying to squeeze new experiences into an already-overfilled day, just trying to keep up while meeting the challenges that hit us every day—all of it can be more than a little intoxicating. For many of us, the busier we are, the more alive we feel. Somehow we have to be weaned off the chaos if we're ever going to accomplish anything that counts for eternity with our lives.

Choosing less activity and smaller places will at first feel like a relief. Finally, we will be able to catch our breath and devote ourselves to what really matters rather than continually reacting to the crisis of the moment. But with time, you will most likely find yourself battling boredom in the slow and monotonous pace. I know from experience. The first time this happened to me, I couldn't believe it. How could I get bored while devoting myself to fulfilling God's eternal plan for my life? *What on earth was wrong with me!* I wondered. As it turned out, I'm normal.

Bernie told me he's felt the same thing. A single father who has always had custody of his two sons, Bernie has worked in the same warehouse for twenty years. He starts work at six every morning and gets off at two in the afternoon. For most of that time he's done essentially the exact same thing in his job. "Some days I can hardly stand the thought of going in," he told me. "But I know I have the perfect job because it lets me be more involved in my sons' lives."

And through the years he has been very involved. By getting off at two, he is always home when his sons get home from school. He's coached their football teams and baseball teams and loved every minute of it. Bernie has worked hard to keep his job from getting in the way of what mattered most to him, but that doesn't mean he hasn't had days where he finds himself bored to death. They happen. But it is a small price to pay for putting his sons above his career.

The Temptation for Laziness

After deciding to stop burning the candle at both ends, you may well find yourself tempted not to light it at all. If we aren't careful, what we like to call downsizing may turn into plain old laziness. You exchange the constant on-the-go chaos for lying around on the couch, accomplishing nothing. As we saw earlier, there are times we need to lie around doing nothing—that's called rest. But a perpetual state of rest isn't a downsized life; it's a wasted life.

Choosing less doesn't mean checking all our drive and ambition at the door. Selfish ambition is a bad thing, but the desire to maximize our lives for the kingdom of God is good. We need to choose less, but we must always be on our guard against the temptation to give into laziness and achieve nothing at all.

Financial Pressure

It won't take long, perhaps as little as a few weeks, before the realization hits you that choosing less really means living with less. Ideas like giving things away and doing without the toys people spend their lives chasing sound great . . . in theory. But eventually, the romantic notions of a smaller, simpler life give way to doing without some of the things you once took for granted.

Choosing to prioritize time together with family and friends rather than working as much overtime as you can not only leads to stronger relationships, it also leads to smaller paychecks. And smaller paychecks mean even less of the things you enjoy in life. Money may not be able to buy happiness, but spending it can be a lot of fun—fun you will soon have to learn to live without when you get serious about making your life small enough to matter.

Many of us look to simplifying our lives as a way of relieving financial stress, and that may well be one of the benefits you will reap. However, you need to go into this with your eyes wide open. There is a financial price to downsizing and simplifying your life. Many couples down-size by having one or the other quit their jobs and become a stay-at-home Mom or Dad.

My wife and I did this when our first child was born. If we had it to do over again, we would. However, living on one income often meant struggling to make ends meet. We didn't feel so happily-ever-after when one of our girls had to have her tonsils out when we were between health insurance plans, meaning we had to pay for the operation out of our own pockets. As I said at the beginning of this chapter, simpler does not mean easier, and this is especially true financially. But then, reaching any goal worth attaining never comes without a cost.

Frustration

A funny thing happens when you put others before yourself: the people for whom you have sacrificed so much—those whom you've invested your life in and served so selflessly—don't often fall at your feet, thanking you for all you've done. From time to time someone will notice and show gratitude, but serving others is a selfless task. Because we're working toward an eternal reward, we know we're operating on a system of delayed results.

But some days this just isn't enough. There are days when trying to accomplish something worthwhile by giving your life away to others just leaves you tired and more than a little grumpy. Moreover, the results aren't always what you'd hoped for. It's not just that the people close to you don't appreciate your efforts, they also often don't respond. And their lives look exactly like they did before you tried to make a difference in them.

Throw all of the above on top of the financial pressure we can feel, and we're left feeling very, very frustrated. Some days we will stand back and wonder if we're wasting our lives. We'll throw up our hands and say, "What's the use?!" When we reach this point, we will find we are in good company. Living in a fallen world pushes all of us to our limits and trying to make a difference in this place just sets us up for frustration. But that doesn't mean our efforts are in vain. The Bible tells us, "So we must not get tired of doing good, for we will reap at the proper time if we don't give up" (Gal. 6:9). We can make an eternal difference in the lives of those around us through hard work and perseverance.

Insignificance

We want our lives to matter—that's what started us on this journey. However, we live in an upside-down world where those who devote their lives to what matters most are usually overlooked. Less may be more on an eternal scale, but in the eyes of the world, a small life is an insignificant life. Turning our backs on money and power and everything else our culture says is so important means those who hold those things will overlook us. In their eyes, we won't matter at all.

At first, being relegated to a nobody isn't a pleasant experience. Yet this is exactly the place we need to be to wield the greatest influence on an eternal scale. The Bible says the first will be last and the last will be first (Matt. 19:30). This simply means that in God's economy, those whose lives accomplish the most are those whose lives were nearly invisible on this earth.

Fred Rogers had a firm handle on this truth when he was asked what the greatest event in American history was. He replied, "I can't say; however, I suspect that like so many 'great' events, it was something very simple and very quiet with little or no fanfare (such as forgiving someone else for a deep hurt), which eventually changed the course of history. The really important 'great' things are never the center stage of life's drama. They're always 'in the wings.' That's why it's so essential for us to be mindful of the humble and the deep rather than the flashy and the superficial."

Worth It in the End

Living a life that matters isn't easy. It demands a steep price not everyone is willing to pay. Jesus faced this same problem. At one point the large crowds that followed Him started thinning out. Jesus' message was just a little too radical for most of them. He kept telling them to do things like surrender everything to follow Him. Rather than stick around, the crowds left, muttering under their breath about Jesus' unreasonable demands. Even some of those who claimed to be His disciples walked away. As they left, Jesus turned to the Twelve and gave them their chance to go as well. But they didn't. Peter spoke for all of them when he said, "Lord, who will we go to? You have the words of eternal life" (John 6:68).

That's the tough choice we also face. Deep inside of us, we long to have our lives count for something that lasts longer than we do. We know this world is temporary. We know nothing lasts. And the longer we live, the more we realize that nothing we can accomplish in this world of time ultimately matters. The only way to find the life for which we are searching is to step out of the world of time and live for eternity. If we are convinced that Jesus died and rose again to give us real life, what other choice do we have? We can waste our lives on that which doesn't last. Or we can pay the price and make our lives count. This world doesn't have what we're looking for. Why then would we live as though it did?

Chapter 16

Constant Sacrifice

*Large tasks require great sacrifice for a moment;
small things require constant sacrifice.*
RICHARD FOSTER, *CELEBRATION OF DISCIPLINE*

||||||||||||||||||||||||||||||||||||||||||||||||||||||

*So let's not allow ourselves to get fatigued
doing good. At the right time we will harvest
a good crop if we don't give up, or quit.*
GALATIANS 6:9 MSG

*E*ach September major league baseball teams expand their
rosters from twenty-five to forty players for the final
month of the season, giving minor league prospects their
first taste of life in the big leagues. Most wind up back in the
minors the following season. From time to time a late season
call-up makes such an impression on the major league club
that they have to keep him around. But few have ever had the
kind of September Shane Spencer put together for the New
York Yankees in 1998.

The Yankees had already established themselves as the
class of the league, setting an American League record with
114 wins on their way to their twenty-fourth World Series
championship. By the time Spencer joined the team, they

had a commanding nineteen-game lead in the standings over the second place Boston Red Sox. The only drama left in the season was whether the Yankees would match the 1906 Chicago Cubs all-time wins record of 116. But all that changed when Spencer began doing his best Mickey Mantle imitation by hitting home runs at a blistering pace. He electrified the Bronx, belting ten home runs in only twenty-seven games and driving in twenty-seven runs. In September he tied a major-league record by hitting three grand slams in one month. His bat stayed hot into the play-offs. In the first round series against the Texas Rangers, he hit two home runs in only six at-bats.

Spencer's power surprised everyone. A twenty-eighth round choice in the 1990 draft, he didn't carry lofty expectations into New York. Just suiting up in pinstripes was an accomplishment in itself. If he had been able to sustain the power he displayed in his first twenty-seven games, Shane Spencer would have become a superstar and a Yankee legend. But his first month in the big leagues was also his best. During the next six seasons he hit only forty-nine home runs. He left the Yankees in 2003, playing for the Indians, the Rangers, and the Mets before returning to the Yankees minor league system in August 2004. Yankee fans will always remember Spencer's magical September of 1998. However, he joined a long line of players who made incredible debuts, but ended up with less than memorable careers.

In the Middle

Anybody can make a good beginning. Few finish well. Fewer still combine a good beginning and ending with a strong middle. When it comes to choosing a life of less, starting off on the right foot isn't the hard part. Neither is ending well. As we near the end of our lives, we're often able to see through the trappings of this world and realize what is truly important in life. The tough part is the in-between.

Downsizing our lives is often like trying to downsize our waistlines. Many of us start diets and exercise routines as New Year's resolutions. We faithfully cut back on fat or carbs or calories or whatever it is we're supposed to cut back on these days to lose weight. During our lunch hours we go to the gym or the park and walk or run or do some sort of exercise. Sticking with the carrots and nonfat yogurt for lunch is tough when everyone else in the office is going to the local Mongolian barbecue, but we resist, just as we resist the cake in the break room someone brought in for the boss's birthday. We refuse to give in because we are determined to eat right, exercise, lose the weight, and get healthier before spring.

Sometimes our resolve lasts until Groundhog Day, but it usually doesn't. A few hardy souls stick with it past Valentine's Day and almost make it to St. Patrick's Day, but most of us fall back to eating Snickers bars and cheese doodles after a week or two. We mean well. Our intentions are sincere, but once the shock of gaining ten pounds during the holidays wears off, sincerity has to give way to discipline before lasting change can take place.

The hectic pace of life takes its toll on everyone from time to time. In an introspective moment we may even look around at our collection of toys and wonder what we're accomplishing with our lives. But real lifestyle change must go much deeper than momentary dissatisfaction with life. We must become convinced that living for eternity and influencing lives in a way that lasts for generations are the only pursuits worthy of a lifetime. This resolve will only get us started down this path. Keeping at it requires determination and daily discipline. Living a life of less must become a habit, not just an occasional bold stroke like giving a large gift to charity once or twice a year. Discipline touches the smallest parts of our lives. That's where this life of less must be lived out.

Service of the Small Things

We started this journey with a simple question: What do you really want out of life? The answer goes beyond finding happiness. All of us want our lives to matter. We want our brief existence on this earth to count for something larger than ourselves. The very thing we seek comes through exerting godly influence in the lives of those around us—an influence that lasts for generations. Simplifying and slowing down our lives helps to clear the obstacles that keep us from reaching our goal. Bringing our material possessions and schedules under God's control is an important step in this process but isn't an end in itself. The purpose in all of this is to make our lives small enough to matter in the lives of those around us.

Living this out on a daily basis demands what Richard Foster calls "the service of small things"[1]—or serving people in the small, mundane details of life few people notice. Dietrich Bonhoeffer called this the service of "active helpfulness."[2] This ministry takes serving others to a whole new level.

Most people, even the most self-absorbed among us, are moved when they see fellow human beings in dire need.

When three consecutive hurricanes hit Florida in 2004, people all over the country collected food and other supplies to send to the storm victims. In the same way, when tsunamis hit Asia during the Christmas holidays in the same year, people around the world sent money to help with the relief efforts.

Faced with tragedy on such an unimaginable scale, the rest of us knew we had to do something. I've seen the same thing take place on a smaller level when a house fire breaks out in a small town. School children organize food and clothes drives, and the whole town rallies around the family in need . . . for a short time.

The service of small things doesn't just give a donation for disaster relief. It moves us to shovel the snow from a neighbor's steps or drive a friend around town running errands when his car is in the shop. When I was a pastor in Indiana, our church sat next to a used car lot. Whenever it snowed (and it snows a lot in Indiana), Tom, the owner of the used car lot, would plow the church's parking lot late at night when no one would notice. The first few times he did this, I had no idea who was behind it. Tom didn't want any recognition, and if I hadn't caught him in the act at ten o'clock one Saturday night, I might never have known he was the phantom plower. This is the service of small things and this is where all of our talk of simplifying and downsizing rises and falls.

The whole point of getting our lives down to a manageable size is to free ourselves from the demands of this world so that we might serve other people. And if we do not serve others in the small things, we do not yet understand what it means to be a servant.

Constant Sacrifice

Several years ago, when I was first sorting through the ideas that eventually grew into this book, I came across a statement by Richard Foster that I've never been able to shake. "Large tasks require great sacrifice for a moment," he wrote in *Celebration of Discipline*, "small things require constant sacrifice."[3] This is, in a nutshell, what it means to choose less to gain more. The lifestyle of choosing less stuff, less activity, less of me, is a lifestyle of constant small sacrifices. Investing my life in the lives of others means more than putting my life on the line and dying for them if I need to. Instead it means making myself available to serve others, even when I would rather do anything else. Perhaps this is what Paul had in mind when he wrote, "And if I donate all my goods to feed the poor, and if I give my body to be burned, but do not have love, I gain nothing" (1 Cor. 13:3).

Great sacrifices demand far less than the day-to-day monotony of loving others enough to put them before myself. Giving everything I have to the poor may inspire others to be more generous, but the impact of that one act cannot compare to a lifetime of giving of my time and my resources in both large and small ways.

Choosing a life of less isn't about getting your financial house in order or restoring order to a chaotic schedule; it is about making your life small enough to matter. And the only way you will is by laying everything aside and making the constant small sacrifices serving others demands. Then when this life is over, you will be able to look back and know that you invested your life wisely. Small sacrifices make a difference that spreads over both time and eternity. They yield a life worth living.

Epilogue

A sterling reputation is better than striking it rich;
a gracious spirit is better than money in the bank.
PROVERBS 22:1 MSG

I hadn't driven this stretch of road in a dozen years—not
since my wife and I drove home from my grandmother's
funeral. I never had a reason to go back after she died. It's
funny how life closes familiar doors. When I was growing
up, my family would drive down Highway 81 a dozen or so
times a year. We'd go south of Chickasha and pass through
Rush Springs, the self-proclaimed watermelon capital of the
world, on our way to Stephens Street in the metropolis of
Marlow, Oklahoma.

And there at the corner of Stephens and Fifth sat the
white two-story house with the green roof where Buck and
Genoa Hervey lived for as long as anyone could remember.
A Pentecostal church sat on the opposite corner, or at least it
did when I was a kid. We'd sit outside on the front porch on
summer evenings and listen as the crowd inside got caught
up in the Spirit. My family spent a lot of time on that porch,
talking, laughing, and watching my grandmother attack wasp
nests armed with a rake and flaming newspaper.

My grandfather died two months before I met my wife.
Seven years later, my grandmother joined him. When she

died, the trips stopped. Like I said, I never had a reason to go back. One year after her funeral, my wife and I watched as movers packed all our worldly possessions into a truck, loaded our two small children into our Nissan Sentra, and moved 1,500 miles away. Five years later we moved again, but we were still more than 800 miles away from the corner of Stephens and Fifth in Marlow, Oklahoma.

Yet one hot afternoon in June 1998, I decided I needed to travel this road one more time. I'd come to the area with a group from my church to put a new roof on a struggling church's building in a tiny town in southwest Oklahoma. We did most of our work early in the morning and late in the evening. As the shingles can't take people walking around on them when the temperature hits triple digits (which it did every day we were there), our afternoons were left free. After spending the first couple of afternoons in the hotel pool, I had the bright idea to go south on Highway 81 to the little town of Marlow to visit my grandparents' graves.

Finding the town was easy. I even had an idea of where to find the cemetery. The last time I was there, I rode in the hearse carrying my grandmother's body. I conducted her funeral and the graveside service. After taking one or two wrong turns, I finally found the cemetery, but nothing looked familiar. I knew I needed help finding the plot where both my grandparents were buried. I went back to Main Street and drove to the First Baptist Church. My grandfather served there as a deacon for decades. He even worked there as a custodian after he retired from farming. Back then I would follow him around during the weeks I stayed with my grandparents during the summers.

I thought someone at the church might now be able to steer me in the right direction. But they couldn't. All of the staff had changed in the past few years. They acted like they recognized the names, but they didn't. However, they suggested I try the local funeral home, which kept a site map of the cemetery. Perhaps they could help me find what I was looking for.

I walked into the Marlow funeral home and told the receptionist what I needed. An old man in a side room overheard the conversation. When I mentioned my grandfather's name, the man walked out and introduced himself, then said, "Buck Hervey. I haven't heard that name in a very long time. I knew him for a lot of years. Went to church together." He paused for a moment then said, "He was probably the finest man I ever met."

Those words kept ringing in my ears when I finally found the graves of my grandparents. The pink marble headstone didn't have any words etched upon it beyond the usual information found on every other headstone in the cemetery. Standing next to his grave, I realized my grandfather had carved his name on hearts, not tombstones. And even though the number of people who remember him has dwindled down to only a handful, his legacy is not diminished. My grandfather had true riches even though he never had much that this world values. The Book of Proverbs says a good name is better than silver or gold. Twenty years after my grandfather had passed away, his riches continued to shine.

As a boy I grew up idolizing my grandfather. He never had much, nor did anyone outside of his circle of family and friends know his name. But he was the man I hoped to become someday. Now, more than twenty-five years after his death, that desire burns brighter than ever. Life isn't about acquiring more or trying to experience everything planet

Notes

Chapter 2: Worth the Effort

1. Ray Bradbury, *Fahrenheit 451* (New York: Ballantine Books, 1989), 157.

2. Francis A. Schaeffer, *No Little People* (Downers Grove, Ill.: InterVarsity Press, 1974), 32.

Chapter 4: Don't Make Me Be Last

1. Taken from the Amazon.com editorial review of *Get Anyone to Do Anything: Never Feel Powerless Again—With Psychological Secrets to Control and Influence Every Situation* by David Lieberman, www.amazon.com/exec/obidos/tg/detail/-/0312270178/ref=pd_sim_b_2/104-1678758-3423142?%5Fencoding=UTF8&v=glance.

2. Walter Bauer, *A Greek-English Lexicon of the New Testament and Other Early Christian Literature*, ed. Frederick William Danker (Chicago: Univ. of Chicago Press, 1979), 486.

3. Richard J. Foster, *Celebration of Discipline: The Path to Spiritual Growth* (New York: HarperCollins, 1998), 132.

Chapter 6: Into Something Beautiful

1. Schaeffer, *No Little People*, 234.

Chapter 7: The Power of Contentment

1. Mark Gongloff, "Consumers Shying Away from Debt," money.cnn.com/2002/10/08/news/economy/consumer_ credit.

2. "Consumers Cautiously Increase Debt," *Houston Chronicle,* 8 February 2005, Business section.

3. Kim Khan, "How Does Your Debt Compare?" *MSN Money* at moneycentral.msn.com/content/SavingandDebt/ P70741.asp.

Chapter 8: But I Live in the Real World

1. Francis A. Schaeffer, *True Spirituality* (Wheaton, Illinois: Tyndale House Publishers, 1971), 19.

2. Foster, *Discipline,* 85.

Chapter 9: Courtney Dreads Christmas

1. Poll commissioned by the Center for a New American Dream and conducted in August 2003 by Widmeyer Research & Polling of Washington, D.C., www.newdream. org/live/time/timepoll.php.

2. Population Reference Bureau, www.prb.org/Content/ NavigationMenu/PRB/Educators/Human_Population/Health2/ World_Health1.htm.

3. *Health, United States, 2004,* compiled by the National Center for Health Statistics (NCHS), Centers for Disease Control and Prevention.

Chapter 10: Time

1. Kurt Wise, *Faith, Form, and Time: What the Bible Teaches and Science Confirms about Creation and the Age of the Universe* (Nashville: Broadman and Holman, 2002), 175–76.

2. Andy Pettitte, Bob Reccord, Mark Tabb, *Strike Zone: Targeting a Life of Integrity and Purity* (Nashville: Broadman and Holman, 2005), 88.

3. Mitch Albom, *Tuesdays with Morrie* (New York: Doubleday, 1997), 64–65.

Chapter 14: Happily Ever After

1. C. S. Lewis, *The Weight of Glory: And Other Addresses* (New York: HarperCollins, 2001), 26.

Chapter 16: Constant Sacrifice

1. Foster, *Discipline*, 135.

2. Dietrich Bonhoeffer, *Life Together* (New York: Harper & Row, 1952), 99.

3. Foster, *Discipline*, 135.